Kernel
Discriminant
Analysis

ELECTRONIC & ELECTRICAL ENGINEERING RESEARCH STUDIES

PATTERN RECOGNITION & IMAGE PROCESSING RESEARCH STUDIES SERIES

Series Editor: **Dr. Josef Kittler,**
Rutherford Appleton Laboratory, England

1. Statistical Pattern Classification using Contextual Information
   K-S Fu *and* **T. S. Yu**

2. Kernel Discriminant Analysis
   D. J. Hand

Kernel Discriminant Analysis

D. J. Hand, M.A.,M.Sc.,Ph.D.

Biometrics Unit, Institute of Psychiatry,
London University, England

RESEARCH STUDIES PRESS
A DIVISION OF JOHN WILEY & SONS LTD
Chichester · New York · Brisbane · Toronto · Singapore

RESEARCH STUDIES PRESS

Editorial Office:
58B Station Road, Letchworth, Herts. SG6 3BE, England

Library of Congress Cataloguing in Publication Data:

Hand, D. J.
   Kernel discriminant analysis.
   (Pattern recognition & image processing series; v.2)
   Includes index.
   1. Discriminant analysis. 2. Pattern perception.
   I. Title.   II. Series
   QA278.65.H37   519.5'35   82-1899
   ISBN 0 471 10211 3   AACR2

British Library Cataloguing in Publication Data:

Hand, D. J.
   Kernel discriminant analysis.—(Pattern recognition
   and image processing research studies series; v.2)
   1. Discriminant analysis
   I. Title   II. Series
   519.5'3   QA278
   ISBN 0 471 10211 3

Printed in Great Britain

Preface

The kernel method of discriminant analysis has benefitted from two different traditions. On the one hand we have the large body of theoretical and practical knowledge constituting statistics, and on the other we have the young and vigorous science called pattern recognition. Thus the kernel method is a dynamic area with an exceptionally well understood mathematical basis and also a wide range of practical problems to its credit. In this book I have attempted to collect together the theory and practice to present both an introduction to the field and a survey of its present state.

One of the difficulties I encountered while working on the book was a consequence of the interest the method arouses. Even as I was writing, new papers - and important and fundamental papers at that, not mere refinements of details - were being published. My apologies to anyone whose paper I may have missed.

I have developed the theory in some detail, quoting the statements of the relevant theorems and proving the most important of these. I have also summarised the simulation results and the real data analyses described in the literature by others, as well as presenting some analyses applied to new sets of real data. Some original material is presented.

It gives me great pleasure to extend my thanks to those who supported me during the preparation of this book. First, I am particularly grateful to Dr. Josef Kittler, the series editor, for giving me the opportunity to collate and publish my thoughts on this fascinating topic. Without his suggestion that I should contribute to the series

(vi)

no doubt the book would have remained a mere half-formed idea at the back of my mind. I am also grateful to those who gave me permission to use their data in analyses described herein, including Dr. Sylvia Dische and the members of the Aircraft Noise Unit and the General Practice Research Unit here at the Institute, as well as to those authors who gave me permission to reproduce their results. The sources are acknowledged in the text. I am grateful to Mr. Nortei Omaboe for producing the excellent graphs in Figures 3.3 to 3.7 using the University of London Computer Centre facilities.

There remain a number of people whose comments, suggestions and support contributed to whatever merits the book may possess. These include Dr. William Yule, Mr. Alan Smith, Mr. Brian Everitt, and Miss Janet Hunter. Naturally I take full responsibility for the faults which remain.

Finally, we come to the two people without whom you would not be reading this book. there is, of course, the typist, Tricia Falconer Smith, who undertook the onerous task of translating page after page of text into camera ready copy, and who did it so beautifully. And last, and perhaps most important of all, we come to my wife, Catherine, who put up with me disappearing into my study almost every evening for the year 1981 to write this book.

October 1981

David Hand,
Institute of Psychiatry,
London University.

Notation

(These are the most common meanings. There may be local variations,
which will be explained when they occur.)

$\underline{x}$	A d-variate vector of measurements on an object.
$f_i(\underline{x})$	The class conditional probability density function for class i (continuous variables).
$f(\underline{x})$	As $f_i(\underline{x})$, but for an arbitrary class, the subscript being dropped for convenience.
π_i	The prior probability for class i.
C_{ij}	The cost of misclassifying an object from class i to class j.
c	The number of classes.
S_j	An object with vector $\underline{x}$ is classified as belonging to class j if $\underline{x}$ lies in the region S_j of R^d.
R	The real line $(-\infty, \infty)$.
$\{\underline{x}_1,\ldots,\underline{x}_n\}$	The design set of a particular class.
n_i or n	The number of design set elements in class i. Sometimes, when there is no risk of confusion, the subscript is dropped.
$\{\underline{x}_1,\ldots,\underline{x}_N\}$	The complete design set.
N	The total number of design set elements $(= n_1+\ldots+n_c)$.
$\hat{f}(\underline{x})$	The density estimate at $\underline{x}$ for an arbitrary class.
K	A kernel function.
h	Smoothing parameter for continuous variables.

(viii)

$f^{(m)}(x)$ m^{th} derivative of $f(x)$.

$f'(x)=f^{(1)}(x)$

$f''(x)=f^{(2)}(x)$

G   Measurement complexity. $G = \prod\limits_{i=1}^{d} g_i$ where g_i is the number of values that the ith categorical variable can take.

$n(\underline{x})$ The number of design set points (for an arbitrary class) falling in cell $\underline{x}$, when $\underline{x}$ is a vector of categorical variables.

$r(\underline{x})$ The multinomial estimate of probability of cell $\underline{x}$. That is, $r(\underline{x}) = n(\underline{x})/n$.

$p(\underline{x})$ The true probability distribution over the G cells of the cross-classification of $\underline{x}$, a vector of categorical variables.

$\hat{\pi}_i(\underline{x})$ Posterior estimate of class membership of $\underline{x}$.

Contents

(x)

CHAPTER 1
Introduction

1.1   BASIC IDEAS

Classification tasks are fundamental to many aspects of human endeavour, including science itself. In many situations, however, the similar nature of different problems may be disguised by the use of words other than "classification", even though the general idea is the same: diagnosis, prognosis, recognition, identification and prediction are examples of such words. This selection of alternative descriptive terms hints at the vast range of areas in which such problems occur. These areas include medicine, psychology, physics, chemistry, archaeology, marine biology, military applications etc. The list is unlimited. The applications may be made in real time (e.g. speech recognition, industrial plant control) or in comfort back in the laboratory (e.g. identifying botanical specimens). A very low risk of error may be essential (e.g. target recognition) or not so vital (e.g. fingerprint identification). The data on which classifications are to be based might be hard (e.g. the physical sciences) or soft (e.g. the social sciences). So we have a huge class of problem areas with differing requirements and differing backgrounds, all of which have a fundamental underlying similarity. This book describes a general method for tackling such problems: the kernel method.

First, let us define more clearly the common nature of the problems we are addressing. There are, broadly speaking, two types of classification problem. On the one hand we have <u>cluster analysis</u>. This is the collective term used to describe methods for imposing a class structure on a set of objects. (For example, one might wish to see if a certain disease was composed of subgroups, or if human languages fell into natural classes). Nothing is assumed to be known about the class memberships of the objects prior to the analysis. Techniques of this sort are most commonly used for exploratory purposes. We are not concerned with cluster analysis.

The other type of classification problem, the type with which we are concerned, begins with a sample (the "design" or "training" sample) of objects of known classification. Thus, a class structure already exists. The aim is then to devise a classification rule for future objects on the basis of the design sample. For example, we might wish to predict the probability of success or failure of a prophylactic surgical operation on the basis of operations we have carried out in the past. This example might suggest that the methods are only applicable to prospective problems but this is not the case. An effective classification procedure might exist, but it might be too slow or too costly to apply. A quicker or cheaper method may be imperative. Or perhaps the existing method might defy automation or be too subjective.

Examples of classification problems of the kind we are concerned with may be found in books on discriminant analysis and pattern recognition (some such are recommended in section 1.3). Pattern recognition has an orientation towards computer science and artificial intelligence (an extreme view in this direction was recently demonstrated by the editor of a pattern recognition newsletter, when she suggested that perhaps machine perception would be a better name) while discriminant analysis has a more traditional statistical basis. However, attempting to delineate the distinction between the two sciences is something of a pointless exercise as their fundamental aims and methods are the same. Perhaps we should point out here that discriminant analysis can also be studied with other aims in mind. Some authors emphasise its use simply to measure the "distinguishability" between classes, while others emphasise its use as a method for interpretation or structural elucidation - finding out what aspects of the objects being studied are important in distinguishing between classes. (This latter usage is particularly important in the social and behavioural sciences.) In this book, however, we concentrate on the classification role.

In the above we have referred to "objects" and "aspects of objects". The time has come to formalise these ideas. An object can be anything: a person to be assigned to a disease class, a disease to be assigned to one of a group of diseases, a word to be recognised as belonging to the ways of pronouncing a particular word, an insect as belonging to a particular species, and so on. For each object we will attempt to assign it to a class by studying the values of measurements made on a number of its attributes. Which measurements are taken will depend on the objects (biochemical measurements in organic medicine, questionnaires in psychology, physical dimensions for archaeological specimens, and so on) and we will preserve the general nature of our study by simply speaking of the "vector of measurements" or the "vector of variables" without specifying in detail what they are.

Clearly we wish to assign the objects to classes in a way which minimises some measure of error. This might be the straightforward misclassification rate or it might be something more sophisticated. For example, let $f_i(\underline{x})$ be the probability density function for class i (or the corresponding function if $\underline{x}$ is categorical), let π_i be the prior probability of class i, and let C_{ij} be the cost of misclassifying an object from class i as class j. Then the overall expected loss is

$$L = \sum_{i=1}^{c} \sum_{j=1}^{c} C_{ij} \int_{S_j} \pi_i f_i(\underline{x}) d\underline{x}$$

where c is the number of classes and where the object with measurement vector $\underline{x}$ is classified as belonging to class j if $\underline{x} \in S_j$. This overall loss is minimised if we choose S_j such that $\underline{x} \in S_j$ whenever

$$\sum_i C_{ij} \pi_i f_i(\underline{x}) < \sum_i C_{ik} \pi_i f_i(\underline{x}) \text{ for all } k \neq j \qquad (1.1.1)$$

The simpler case referred to above, when we wish to minimise the misclassification rate, occurs when

$$C_{ij} = \begin{array}{l} 1 \quad \text{if } i \neq j \\[10pt] 0 \quad \text{if } i = j \end{array}$$

If we knew the π_i and $f_i(\underline{x})$ there would be no problem. We could calculate

$$\sum_i C_{ij} \pi_i f_i(\underline{x})$$

for j = 1,...,c and find the smallest. $\underline{x}$ would then be allocated to this class with the smallest value. Usually, however, the π_i and $f_i(\underline{x})$ are not known. They must somehow be estimated from the design set. Estimation of the π_i is usually (at least in principle) straightforward, and the difficulty lies with estimating the $f_i(\underline{x})$. In the next section we very briefly survey methods for doing this. Note that this formulation means we can often consider classes individually rather than simultaneously ("often" rather than "always" because practical advantages sometimes follow if we do the latter - as will be evident below).

1.2   METHODS

A large number of methods of discriminant analysis and pattern recognition have been proposed. They are surveyed in Hand (1981b). The early work tended to assume interval scale measurements and it is only recently, and primarily in discriminant analysis rather than pattern recognition, that a corresponding development has taken place for categorical data. This probably reflects a general trend throughout multivariate statistics and is in part a consequence of the development of the computer, a point to which we return below.

The earliest discriminant analysis method to be developed (and still the one most widely used in practice) is the linear discriminant function method of Fisher. Linearity is a ubiquitous assumption in multivariate statistics, its simplicity and mathematical elegance often outweighing the fact that it might be suboptimal. Fisher's method makes no explicit assumptions about the forms of the class conditional distributions but merely finds the hyperplanar surface ("decision surface") which best separates the classes, where best is defined in terms of a function of estimated class means and covariance matrices. However, one of the reasons for the importance of the method is that for two normal distributions with identical covariance matrices the optimal decision surface is indeed linear and if the mean and covariance estimators are chosen properly the Fisher method will converge to this optimal decision surface.

The criterion introduced by Fisher is only one which may be used to determine the "best" linear decision surface. Others have been introduced by the pattern recognition fraternity, where the emphasis has often been on speed and ease of computation. The perceptron criterion is one such.

Of course, linearity may often be too severe a restriction to impose on the decision surface form and more flexible surfaces might be required. One way to achieve greater flexibility is to generalise the linear form and use piecewise linear decision surfaces - decision surfaces composed of many small linear segments. Another way is to use linear functions of non-linear functions of the original measurements. Obviously this latter approach permits arbitrary complexity. An example is the quadratic decision surface extension of the classical linear discriminant function method. Such a decision surface is optimal for two normal classes with covariance matrices which are not necessarily equal. It is worth making a cautionary comment here that introducing an arbitrarily large number of parameters is not without a concomitant cost. This is obviously true in terms of increased computational requirements, but it is also true in terms of the precision with which the parameters can be estimated. This is a point to which we return later in this book.

Another way of generalising the basic linear method is to transform a linear function of the measurements. The logistic method is of this type. This particular method has the property that not only is it optimally matched to the two normal class equal covariance matrix case, but also to some categorical variable cases.

The discussion above has focussed on estimating parameters which define the decision surface. We could reformulate this in terms of parameters defining the class conditional distributions. The above methods then take the chosen family of distributions and substitute estimates for their parameters in the optimal decision rule (1.1.1). An alternative approach is the Bayesian one. If $f(\underline{x}|\underline{\theta})$ is the family of distributions for one of the classes, indexed by parameter vector $\underline{\theta}$, then we can obtain a posterior distribution for $f(\underline{x}|\underline{x}_1,\ldots,\underline{x}_n)$ (the distribution of $\underline{x}$ given the design set $\{\underline{x}_1,\ldots,\underline{x}_n\}$ for this class) as

$$f(\underline{x}|\underline{x}_1,\ldots,\underline{x}_n) = \int f(\underline{x}|\underline{\theta})r(\underline{\theta}|\underline{x}_1,\ldots,\underline{x}_n)d\underline{\theta}$$

$$= \int f(\underline{x}|\underline{\theta}) \frac{L(\underline{x}_1,\ldots,\underline{x}_n|\underline{\theta})r(\underline{\theta})}{\int L(\underline{x}_1,\ldots,\underline{x}_n|\underline{\theta})r(\underline{\theta})d\underline{\theta}} d\underline{\theta}$$

where L is the likelihood function of the design set and $r(\underline{\theta})$ is the prior distribution of $\underline{\theta}$. In some situations $r(\underline{\theta}|\underline{x}_1,\ldots,\underline{x}_n)$ takes the same form as $r(\underline{\theta})$ and we can simply substitute new values for the parameters but in general computational problems will be encountered with this method.

The Bayesian method, in common with the earlier methods, assumes that the class conditional distributions (or, at least, the decision surfaces) belong to a certain family of functions. Nonparametric approaches relax this restriction.

Two major methods of nonparametric discriminant analysis exist, though they are very closely connected. One can regard them as generalisations of the traditional histogram density estimate. A major obstacle in using the histogram for discriminant analysis is the inordinately large number of cells if d (the number of variables) is even moderate. With the fixed cell structure of the histogram this can only be avoided by having cells which are very large - not accurately reflecting local variations in density. The kernel and nearest neighbour methods avoid the problem by permitting the cell structure to move. To be precise, the density at a point is estimated from a cell located at that point. The nearest neighbour method fixes the number, k, of design set points and finds the volume which contains the nearest k. From this number and volume the density may be estimated. The kernel method, on the other hand, fixes the volume and finds the number in this volume. Again these two values lead to a density estimate. In fact for purposes of classification nearest neighbour and kernel methods rather more sophisticated than the crude methods described above are used. This book describes the kernel methods. Nearest neighbour methods are described in more detail in Hand (1981b).

  The order in which the methods have been described above roughly reflects the order in which they were developed. The first descriptions of methods which are now called kernel methods seem to be those of Fix and Hodges (1951), Rosenblatt (1956), and Parzen (1962). The late development of the nonparametric methods is at least partly, if not almost entirely, due to their fundamental arithmetic intractability compared to the parametric forms. It is only the advent of the computer which has made such methods practically feasible. Although they may have been developed only recently, however, the interest shown in such methods has more than made up for this. This is demonstrated by Fig. 1.1 which is a histogram by years of the publications listed in the comprehensive bibliography of density estimation prepared by Wertz and Schneider (1979). (The decline in numbers at the far right of the diagram is presumably due to the publications not having been unearthed, rather than a real effect!) The kernel method in particular seems to stimulate interest, both from theoretically minded mathematical statisticians and from applications oriented consultant statisticians.

A natural question when one is confronted with the evident enthusiasm for this class of methods is: why? What do these methods have that other, more traditional methods do not? The most immediate answer is that in nonparametric discriminant analysis the class conditional distribution estimates and the decision surfaces are more flexible than in traditional methods. The data plays a much more prominent role in the former than in the latter, where the permissible forms for estimated distributions and decision surfaces are straitjacketed by the a priori assumptions about the parametric families. (In fact things are not as bad as this might seem to imply. Traditional methods are well suited to particular types of problem - though mis-use is common).

In addition to this, there is a more fundamental kind of inherent flexibility possessed by kernel methods. They can be easily adapted to different types of problem. For example, categorical variables are common in certain sciences (e.g. social sciences and medicine) and kernel methods can be used with these just as easily as with continuous interval scale variables. Indeed, they can equally easily be applied to problems involving mixtures of variable types. Moreover kernel

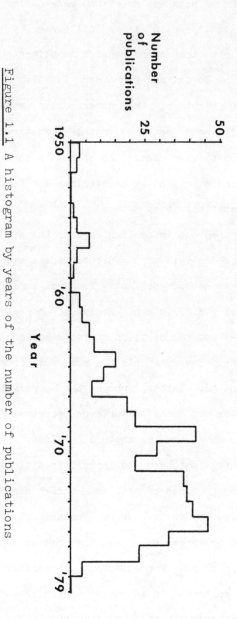

Figure 1.1 A histogram by years of the number of publications
on statistical density estimation listed in Wertz and Schneider (1979).

methods lead to their classifications via probability estimates. This makes it easy to implement the reject option and other refinements of the fundamental classification algorithm, as discussed later in this book.

Kernel methods have well understood mathematical properties, as is evident from a perusal of any of the survey articles listed in the next section. Because of their youth, however, kernel discriminant analysis methods have yet to be widely applied to practical problems. Certainly nowhere near as many studies have been published describing the use of kernel discriminant analysis as have been published describing the use of Fisher's linear discriminant function. The forty year head start of the latter is responsible for this. (Another consequence of this same cause is that Fisher's method is the most widely programmed method in computer packages.) The youth of kernel discriminant analysis means that it is a rich field for further research, especially on the more applications oriented side.

1.3   BACKGROUND READING

Background reading for this book falls conveniently into two classes. On the one hand we have more general studies of discriminant analysis and pattern recognition methods, and on the other hand we have studies of nonparametric probability density function estimation, especially kernel estimation.

A recent book in the first group is Hand (1981b). This begins with an introduction to decision theory and proceeds through nonparametric and parametric methods. Other chapters deal with linear discriminant functions, discrete variables, variable selection, and cluster analysis. The various methods are illustrated by examples on real data. The orientation is towards statisticians rather than pattern recognition scientists but unlike other statistical books an attempt has been made to cover the whole spectrum of discriminant analysis methods.

Other books with a statistical orientation include Lachenbruch (1975), Goldstein and Dillon (1978), and Klecka (1980). The first is a study of classical linear discriminant analysis. It provides a useful introduction to this subject, though little information comparing the classical method with any of the others outlined in the preceding section or considered in Hand (1981b). The bibliography of 579 references would be useful for anyone beginning research in the area.

Goldstein and Dillon (1978) surveys methods of discriminant analysis on categorical variables. The book is really a summary of papers published before it was written and does little to digest them. For some unaccountable reason it omits mention of the kernel method apart from a reference to Hills's approach (see Chapter 4 of the present work). A more extensive but less detailed outline of methods of discriminant analysis which may be applied to a particular type of categorical data problem is contained in Hand (1981a), which considers multivariate binary data.

Klecka (1980), like Lachenbruch (1975), concentrates on classical discriminant analysis. Klecka also wrote the discriminant analysis chapter in the SPSS program manual (Nie et al, 1975) and Klecka (1980) describes in detail how to interpret the output of such a program. The book is non-technical and I would thoroughly recommend it to anyone using a classical discriminant analysis program who wishes to obtain a basic understanding of the method.

Turning from statistically oriented to pattern recognition oriented books, we find a slight shift in emphasis (for example, one aspect of this shift is less emphasis on significance tests and more emphasis on computational aspects). Early works include Fukunaga (1972), Meisel (1972), and Tou and Gonzales (1974). Fukunaga (1972) remains an excellent introductory text although, as is commonly the case with pattern recognition books, it devotes little attention to categorical data (and what attention there is is largely confined to binary variables - this must reflect the electronics/computer science background of pattern recognition). Meisel (1972) and Tou and Gonzales (1974) also have the computational - one might even say electronic hardware - orientation. Tou and Gonzales (1974) includes a chapter on syntactic pattern recognition. Other general pattern recognition texts include Duda and Hart (1973) and Young and Calvert (1974). As well as presenting general surveys of pattern recognition methodology these books also concentrate on particular problem areas.

There is also an increasing number of sets of conference proceedings from both the statistical discriminant analysis and the pattern recognition communities being published as books.

Turning to nonparametric estimation of probability density functions we have the books by Wertz (1978) and Tapia and Thompson (1978). The first of these presents a fairly comprehensive list of theorems relating to nonparametric probability density estimation, tying them together in the text. Proofs are not presented. Theorems relating to the kernel method occupy 34 of the 90 pages of text. The book is very much a survey - as the title describes it - and as a text for a student course a better book is Tapia and Thompson (1978). This begins with "an early statistical investigation - namely, Moses's census of 1490 BC" and works its way forward through kernel estimation to maximum penalised likelihood estimation.

There are also several survey papers on nonparametric probability density estimation, including Wegman (1972) and Fryer (1977). Other comparative studies between methods will be mentioned in later chapters. Finally, there is the comprehensive bibliography on statistical density estimation of Wertz and Schneider (1979).

CHAPTER 2
Kernel Estimators

2.1   INFORMAL CONCEPTS OF KERNEL ESTIMATION

In order to introduce the concepts underlying kernel estimation in a simple way, we begin this chapter with a section illustrating different ways of looking at such estimators. Furthermore, to retain simplicity, we shall temporarily abandon any attempt at generality and shall consider only univariate spaces with continuous variables. That is, each object has only a single measurement taken on it and this measurement can take any value in a certain (possibly finite) range.

As noted in Chapter 1, we can concentrate on a single class. Let the design sample from this class be $\{x_1,\ldots,x_n\}$. Our aim, then, is to find an estimate, $\hat{f}(x)$, of the class conditional probability density function (pdf) $f(x)$ at an arbitrary point x, based on $\{x_1,\ldots,x_n\}$.

The most basic form of nonparametric density estimator is the histogram. This has a number of disadvantages, amongst which are the fixed nature of the cell structure, the discontinuities at cell boundaries, and the fact that it is zero outside a certain range. The first of these properties means that points some distance apart but within the same cell have the same estimated density whereas points near to each other but on different sides of a cell boundary can have very different estimates. In 1956 Murray Rosenblatt used ideas analogous to those of the moving average of time series analysis to alleviate these problems. Instead of having a fixed cell structure, independent of the position of x, the point at which we wish to estimate the density, he suggested centering a cell at x. As with a histogram the probability that a point will fall in the cell centred at x is estimated by the proportion of design set points (for this class) which fall in this cell. The probability density at x is this total probability divided by the volume of the cell (in our case here the volume is the length since we are currently considering only a single variable). Thus if the cell is of length 2h:

$$\hat{f}(x) = \frac{1}{n} \sum_{i=1}^{n} K_1(x-x_i) / 2h \qquad (2.1.1)$$

where

$$K_1(u) = \begin{cases} 1 & \text{if } |u| < h \\ 0 & \text{if } |u| >= h \end{cases}$$

An estimate more closely representing the distribution of the sample results. Figures 2.1 and 2.2 illustrate, respectively, a histogram and the Rosenblatt kernel estimate for the same sample.

The problems are certainly alleviated by this, but they are certainly not entirely solved. Although the steps in the density estimate have been reduced, they still exist.

Another way of looking at (2.1.1) leads to an idea of how we may proceed further. The estimate $\hat{f}(x)$ in (2.1.1) can be viewed as an average of n values, one corresponding to each of the design set points. Points near to x (within distance h) contribute a value 1/2h while points further from x contribute a value 0. It is clearly the

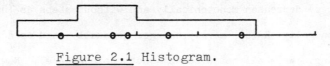

Figure 2.1 Histogram.

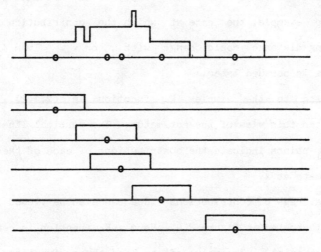

Figure 2.2 Rosenblatt kernel estimate.

jump from 1/2h to 0 which leads to the discontinuities. Thus we could replace $K_1/2h$ by another function $K_2(x-x_i)$ which decreases gradually with increasing $|x-x_i|$. Our estimate then becomes

$$\hat{f}(x) = \frac{1}{n} \sum_{i=1}^{n} K_2(x-x_i) \qquad (2.1.2)$$

where $K_2(u)$ decreases monotonically and without steps as $|u|$ increases (more generally, $K_2(u)$ merely changes gradually and is not monotonic decreasing. We shall not discuss such choices here). Now in regions with many x_i's there will be many large contributions while in regions with few x_i's there will be few large contributions. Note that this can be generalised even further by letting K_2 be a more complicated function of x and x_i, rather than simply of the distance between them. Thus, for example, the rate at which the contribution fell off with increasing distance could change with x or x_i. Then $K_2 = K_2^*(x,x_i)$. This idea is pursued later.

Returning to the simple K_2 function in (2.1.2), Figure 2.3 illustrates this view of the estimator. The vertical lines above each of the x_i points indicate the contributions of each of these points to the estimate at x.

This "average of contributions" idea can also be viewed another way, as is illustrated in Figure 2.4. Here a K_2 function is centred at each design set point. The value of each of these functions at x is its contribution to $\hat{f}(x)$.

Note that if K_2 has the whole real line as its support then the third disadvantage of the histogram – the lack of tails – is removed (although not completely, since the thickness of the tails will depend on the particular K_2 chosen).

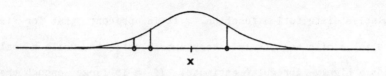

<u>Figure 2.3</u> The contributions of each sample point
to the estimate at x.

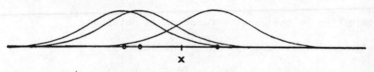

<u>Figure 2.4</u> A kernel centred at each sample point.

Returning, for the moment, to the Rosenblatt kernel of (2.1.1), this can be rewritten as

$$\hat{f}(x) = \{F_n(x+h) - F_n(x-h)\}/2hn \qquad (2.1.3)$$

where $F_n(x)$ is the sample cumulative distribution function. From this $\hat{f}$ can be seen to be an approximation to the derivative of the sample cumulative distribution function. It is apparent that for fixed n a large value of h results in a very smooth estimate, while a small value yields a highly irregular estimate. If h is large enough the entire set $\{x_1,\ldots,x_n\}$ lies within the cell and a uniform estimate results. In the limit as $h \to 0$, which would correspond to $\hat{f}$ being the derivative of the sample cumulative distribution function, $\hat{f}$ would become a series of spikes of probability, one situated at each of the x_i. Such estimates would be useless for the comparative requirements of classification since everywhere except on a set of measure zero the estimate would be zero. By taking $h > 0$ a more tractable and useful approximation to the density function is obtained.

The general form (2.1.2) can be rewritten as

$$\hat{f}(x) = \int K(x-y) dF_n(y) \qquad (2.1.4)$$

which makes it obvious that $\hat{f}$ is a convolution smoothing of the sample cumulative distribution function F_n. Put another way, the smoothing makes operational the intuitively desirable idea that points x near to design set points should have about the same probability of occurring as those design set points. We are thus imposing some kind of restriction on the irregularity of f that our estimate can follow - an assumption that the derivative of f is never too great.

This brings us to another difficulty associated with the histogram and one to which we have not yet referred. This is the problem of choosing the size of the cells. Unfortunately the adoption of the kernel method does not resolve this difficulty. It will be evident from the discussion above that a kernel analogue of the cell size must be chosen with a view to specifying how much irregularity we feel we can model. This will also depend on the sample size, n. We call this analogue the smoothing parameter and denote it by h for continuous variables. When necessary we shall make explicit the dependence of the estimate on h by adopting the general form

$$f(x) = \frac{1}{nh} \sum_{i=1}^{n} K(\frac{x-x_i}{h})$$ (2.1.5)

A considerable effort has been expended on studying ways to find a suitable h, and this is discussed in Chapter 3.

As a final note it is worth commenting that, for our purposes, the kernel method removes yet another disadvantage of the basic histogram approach. This disadvantage, which would render the use of the histogram impracticable for our purposes in most real problems, is the exponential increase in the number of cells as d, the number of variables, increases. The problem has become known as the "curse of dimensionality". The kernel estimate is always simply an average of n contributions, no matter how many variables are involved.

2.2   SINGLE CONTINUOUS VARIABLES

In this section we establish some fundamental mathematical properties of the basic univariate kernel estimators on the real line. In the next section we shall generalise to the more important (to us) multivariate case.

First note that if we restrict the kernel K so that

$$\int K(x)dx = 1$$

and

$$K(x) >= 0 \text{ for all } x$$

then the estimate defined in (2.1.5) also satisfies these properties. Thus, if K is a probability density function so also will $\hat{f}$ be. Sometimes this may be an advantage but it is worth remarking that neither the unit integral nor the non-negative property of $\hat{f}$ are necessary for our purpose. As explained in Chapter 1, our aim is merely to compare probability estimates and this can be done whatever the integral and even if $\hat{f}$ is negative.

We begin by considering bias properties of the estimator $\hat{f}$. First we have the following early theorem due to Rosenblatt.

Theorem 2.2.1: (Rosenblatt, 1956). Let $X_1,\ldots,X_n$ be independent and identically distributed random variables with continuous density function $f(x)$. Let $\hat{f}(x;X_1,\ldots,X_n)$ be an estimate of $f(x)$ which is symmetric in $(x_1,\ldots,x_n)$ and is jointly Borel measurable in $(x,x_1,\ldots,x_n)$ and for which

$$\hat{f}(x;x_1,\ldots,x_n) >= 0.$$

Then $\hat{f}(x;X_1,\ldots,X_n)$ is not an unbiased estimator of $f(x)$ for all $f(x)$. Proof: Suppose to the contrary that

$$E\{\hat{f}(x;X_1,\ldots,X_n)\} \equiv f(x)$$

for all continuous f and for all x. Then

$$E\{\hat{f}(x;X_1,\ldots,X_n)\} < \infty \text{ for all } x.$$

Thus $\int_a^b \hat{f}(x;X_1,\ldots,X_n)dx$ is an unbiased estimator of

$$F(b) - F(a)$$

where F is the cumulative distribution function of x. But, since the symmetrised n-tuple $(X_1,\ldots,X_n)$ is a complete statistic, the only unbiased estimate of $F(b) - F(a)$ symmetric in $X_1,\ldots,X_n$ is

$$F_n(b) - F_n(a)$$

where $F_n(x)$ is the sample distribution function. Thus

$$F_n(b) - F_n(a) = \int_a^b \hat{f}(x;X_1,\ldots,X_n)dx$$

for all a and b and almost all $X_1,\ldots,X_n$. This implies that $F_n(x)$ is absolutely continuous in x for almost all $X_1,\ldots,X_n$, which is impossible.

Rosenblatt also notes that the non-negativity of $\hat{f}$ is not a necessary condition, pointing out that a condition such as

$$\int_a^b E|\hat{f}(x;X_1,\ldots,X_n)|dx < \infty$$

for some a and b, $a < b$, would lead to the same result. Thus there is no non-negative estimator which is unbiased for all continuous $f(x)$. In particular, there is no kernel estimator with non-negative kernel which is unbiased for all continuous $f(x)$.

Yamato (1972) proves an interesting complement to this theorem. Instead of looking for estimators which are unbiased over the whole class of continuous $F(x)$, he considers a particular f and concentrates on kernel estimators with kernels K being probability density functions.

Theorem 2.2.2: (Yamato, 1972). Let $X_1,\ldots,X_n$ be independently and identically distributed random variables with a probability density function $f(x)$. Let K be a measurable function satisfying

$$K(x) >= 0 \text{ for all } x \in R$$

$$\int_R K(x)dx = 1 \tag{2.2.1}$$

where R is the real line. Then the kernel estimator (2.1.2)

is biased. Proof: Again this is proved by assuming it to be true and demonstrating a contradiction. So, suppose there does exist some K satisfying the conditions of the theorem and such that

$$E \{\hat{f}(x)\} = f(x) \text{ for all x.}$$

That is

$$\int_R K(x-y) \ f(y)dy = f(x) \text{ for all x.} \qquad (2.2.2)$$

By the convolution theorem for Fourier transforms we have

$$\phi_{K*f}(u) = \phi_K(u)\phi_f(u) \qquad (2.2.3)$$

where $\phi_g(u)$ is the Fourier transform of function g and K*f is the convolution of K and f. Thus, from (2.2.2) and (2.2.3)

$$\phi_K(u)\phi_f(u) = \phi_f(u) \qquad (2.2.4)$$

Since $\phi_f(u)$ is continuous and equal to 1 at u = 0 there exists some $\delta > 0$ such that

$$\phi_f(u) \neq 0 \text{ for } u \in (-\delta,\delta).$$

Thus from (2.2.4)

$$\phi_K(u) = 1 \text{ for } u \in (-\delta,\delta).$$

Thus, by proposition (a) of Loève (1960) p. 202,

$$\phi_K(u) = 1 \text{ for all } u \in R. \qquad (2.2.5)$$

Since no K exists which simultaneously satisfies (2.2.1) and (2.2.5) we have a contradiction.

Thus in general, for finite samples and with non-negative kernel estimates, it seems that we must accept a certain bias in our estimate (but see below). But what about the asymptotic case? As is common with many other areas of statistics, considerable effort has been expended on establishing asymptotic results. From here on we shall in general content ourselves with merely giving the statements of most of the theorems, omitting the proofs. Readers interested in the details of the proofs can turn to the quoted references.

For our first asymptotic result on bias we have:

Theorem 2.2.3: (Shapiro, 1969) Let $f \in L^1(-\infty,\infty)$ and let K satisfy

$$K \in L^1(-\infty,\infty)$$

$$\int_R K(x)dx = 1.$$

Then if $h \to 0$ as $n \to \infty$

$$\int_R |E\{\hat{f}(x)\} - f(x)|dx \to 0 \text{ as } n \to \infty.$$

Similarly, we can show uniform convergence of $E\{\hat{f}(x)\}$ to $f(x)$:

Theorem 2.2.4: (Shapiro, 1969). Let f be uniformly continuous and bounded on R and let K and h be as in theorem 2.2.3. Then

$$\sup_x |f(x) - E\{\hat{f}(x)\}| \to 0 \text{ as } n \to \infty.$$

For pointwise convergence of the bias to zero we have:

Theorem 2.2.5: (Parzen, 1962). Suppose $K(x)$ is a Borel function satisfying

$$\sup_R |K(x)| < \infty$$

$$\int_R K(x)dx = 1$$

$$\lim_{x \to \infty} |xK(x)| = 0$$

and suppose that $f(x)$ with absolutely continuous distribution function satisfies

$$\int_R |f(x)| dx < \infty.$$

Then if $\lim_{n \to \infty} h = 0$ the kernel estimate defined by (2.1.5) is

asymptotically unbiased at all points of continuity of $f(x)$.

Theorems 2.2.3 to 2.2.5 establish conditions under which different
types of convergence of the bias will occur. In Chapter 3, where we
study the choice of K, rate of convergence of the bias will be of
interest. Shapiro (1969) shows:

Theorem 2.2.6: (Shapiro, 1969). Let K satisfy

$$K(x) \in L^1(-\infty,\infty)$$

$$x^2K(x) \in L^1(-\infty,\infty)$$

$$\int xK(x)dx = 0.$$

Also let $\lim_{n\to\infty} h = 0$ and assume that f is a bounded measurable

absolutely continuous function with $f''(x)$ existing. Then

$$\lim_{n\to\infty} \frac{1}{h^2} b\{\hat{f}(x)\} = -\tfrac{1}{2}\int x^2K(x)dx f''(x) \qquad (2.2.6)$$

where we have put $b\{\hat{f}(x)\} = f(x) - E\{\hat{f}(x)\}$ for the bias of
$\hat{f}(x)$.

All non-negative even kernels with $x^2K \in L^1$ satisfy this result.
Note that when K is restricted to being non-negative

$$\int_R x^2K(x)dx >= 0$$

always so that the bias cannot decrease faster than h^2. Of course, it
may decrease less fast than this. In fact we have from Shapiro (1969):

Theorem 2.2.7: (Shapiro, 1969). Suppose f is bounded and
measurable on R and suppose that $J(f;x)$, defined by

$$J(f;x) = \frac{1}{\pi}\int_0^\infty \frac{f(x+t) - 2f(x) + f(x-t)}{t^2}dt$$

exists as a Lebesgue integral for some particular value of x.
Let $\lim_{n\to\infty} h = 0$. Then

(i) if K is the Cauchy kernel

$$K(x) = \{\pi(1+x^2)\}^{-1}$$

then $\lim_{n\to\infty} b\ \{\hat{f}(x)\}/h = -J(f;x)$.

(ii) if K is the Fejer-de la Vallee Poussin kernel

$$K(x) = (\sin^2 x)/\pi x^2$$

then $\lim_{n\to\infty} b\ \{\hat{f}(x)\}/h = -\frac{1}{2}J(f;x)$.

We have already commented that for our particular application the estimated $\hat{f}(x)$ need not be constrained to be non-negative. Thus we might consider taking $K(x) < 0$ for some x. We could then exercise this extra flexibility in K by choosing K so that

$$\int x^2 K(x) dx = 0$$

(see Bartlett, 1963). From (2.2.6) this would seem to imply an apparently zero bias. But, of course (2.2.6) is an asymptotic result and we must take into account the higher order terms. Generalising the expansion which led to theorem (2.2.6), we have

$$b\ \{\hat{f}(x)\} = -\sum_{r=1}^{m} \frac{h^r(n)}{r!} f^{(r)}(x)\ \int_R z^r K(z) dz + 0\ \{h^{m+1}(n)\}\ (2.2.7)$$

leading to

Theorem 2.2.8: (Shapiro, 1969). Let K satisfy

$$K(x) \in L^1(-\infty,\infty)$$

$$x^m K(x) \in L^1(-\infty,\infty)$$

$$\int x^r K(x) dx = 0 \text{ for } r = 1,\ldots,m-1$$

and let $\int x^m K(x) dx \neq 0$. Then if f is bounded, measurable, and if $f^{(m)}(x)$ exists and $\lim_{n\to\infty} h = 0$ then

$$\lim_{n\to\infty} b\ \{\hat{f}(x)\} = -h^m f^{(m)}(x)\ \int x^m K(x) dx/m!$$

Thus, although the bias is not zero, the rate of convergence to zero as n increases (and h shrinks) is improved if we permit K to take negative values.

For particular f(x) it may be possible to find kernel functions for which the estimator is unbiased. Yamato (1972) gives an example of such an f and K pair. Obviously this is of more theoretical than practical interest since f must be known in order to choose the K.

An interesting paper on more general aspects of unbiased density estimators is Seheult and Quesenberry (1971).

The study of bias alone is all very well but an unbiased estimator or one with a small bias would be of little practical value if it had a large variance. In such a case one would have little confidence that an estimate $\hat{f}(x)$ was near to f(x). Thus we must also consider the variance of the estimator, defined by

$$V \{\hat{f}(x)\} = E \{\hat{f}(x) - E\{ \hat{f}(x)\}\}^2.$$

We begin with a theorem on the asymptotic variance of $\hat{f}(x)$.

Theorem 2.2.9: (Parzen, 1962). Under the conditions of theorem 2.2.5

$$\lim_{n \to \infty} nh\ V \{\hat{f}(x)\} = f(x)\int K^2(x)dx.$$

Murthy (1965) relaxes the requirement that F be absolutely continuous in theorems 2.2.5 and 2.2.9.

We have now examined two measures, the bias and the variance, both of which should be small for a good estimator. The natural next step is to combine them to yield a single measure. This can then be used as a criterion function which we can attempt to optimise by choice of h and K (Chapter 3). We begin by taking the result on bias given by theorem 2.2.6 (i.e. the special case of m = 2 in theorem 2.2.8) and combining this with the result on variance in theorem 2.2.9. This gives the mean square error (MSE)

$$MSE = E \{f(x) - \hat{f}(x)\}^2$$

$$= V \{\hat{f}(x)\} + b^2\{\hat{f}(x)\}$$

$$\rightarrow \frac{f(x)}{nh} \int K^2(y)dy + \frac{h^4 f''(x)^2}{4} \{\int x^2 K(x)dx\}^2 \qquad (2.2.8)$$

as $n \rightarrow \infty$.

It is evident from (2.2.8) that if we choose h such that

$$h \rightarrow 0 \text{ as } n \rightarrow \infty$$

$$\text{and } nh \rightarrow \infty \text{ as } n \rightarrow \infty$$

$$\text{then MSE} \rightarrow 0 \text{ as } n \rightarrow \infty.$$

That is, under the conditions on f and K needed in deriving (2.2.8) and under the above conditions on h, $\hat{f}(x)$ is pointwise consistent in quadratic mean.

Pointwise consistency is all very well, but much more useful are global measures. In particular, the mean integrated squared error (MISE), defined by

$$MISE = E\int \{\hat{f}(x) - f(x)\}^2 dx = \int E \{\hat{f}(x) - f(x)\}^2 dx$$

has been widely used (Rosenblatt, 1971). From the MSE above we get, assuming f'' is integrable,

$$MISE \rightarrow \frac{1}{nh} \int K^2(y)dy + \frac{h^4}{4} \int f''(y)^2 dy \{\int y^2 K(y)dy\}^2$$

as $n \rightarrow \infty$. As before, for the purposes of discrimination and pattern recognition we need not restrict $\hat{f}(x) >= 0$, and advantages in terms of MISE convergence rate can follow if we relax the $K(x) >= 0$ restriction. Nadaraya (1974) has combined the results on convergence of the bias with these more general K (theorem 2.2.8) with the results on convergence of the variance, to yield:

Theorem 2.2.10: (Nadaraya, 1974; referred to in Wertz, 1978). Let f be m times differentiable (m >= 2), $f^{(m)}$ be bounded and square integrable. Let K be an even bounded function with

$$\int K(x)dx = 1$$
$$\int x^r K(x)dx = 0 \text{ for } r = 1,\ldots,m-1$$
$$\int x^m K(x)dx \neq 0$$
$$\int |x^m K(x)|dx < \infty$$

(c.f. theorem 2.2.8). Then

$$\text{MISE} = \frac{1}{nh}\int K^2(x)dx + \frac{h^{2m}}{(m!)^2} \{\int x^m K(x)dx\}^2 \int \{f^{(m)}(x)\}^2 dx$$
$$+ o \{\frac{1}{nh} + h^{2m}\}.$$

We shall make use of this result in chapter 3 when we discuss choice of kernel shape and smoothing parameter.

Apart from the above results of pointwise consistency and consistency in quadratic mean (MSE, MISE $\to$ 0 as n $\to \infty$) other authors have established other kinds of consistency under various conditions. In particular attention has been focussed on uniform consistency. In fact, from Parzen's original (1962) paper we have the following result:

Theorem 2.2.11: (Parzen, 1962). If h $\to$ 0 and $nh^2 \to$ 0 as n $\to \infty$ and if f is uniformly continuous then for all $\delta > 0$

$$P \{\sup_R |\hat{f}(x) - f(x)| < \delta\} \to 1 \text{ as } n \to \infty.$$

Nadaraya (1965) proves the following stronger result:

Theorem 2.2.12: (Nadaraya, 1965). Suppose K(x) is a function of bounded variation, f(x) is a uniformly continuous density function and the series

$$\sum_{n=0}^{\infty} \exp \{-\gamma nh^2\}$$

converges for every positive value of γ. Then

$$\sup_R |\hat{f}(x) - f(x)| \to 0$$

with probability 1 as $n \to \infty$.

A result similar to Nadarya's is presented by Van Ryzin (1969) and for a large class of kernels Schuster (1969) proves conversely that if $\hat{f}$ converges uniformly to f with probability 1 then f must be uniformly continuous.

B.W. Silverman has made some important contributions to kernel estimation, not least of which is his application of the methods to real data sets (see, for example, Silverman, 1978a). This is a welcome contrast to the heavy emphasis on pure theory which has characterised the field in the past. In Silverman (1978) he extended Nadarya's result (theorem 2.2.12, above) by weakening the condition on h, proving:

Theorem 2.2.13: (Silverman, 1978). Let K be uniformly continuous, of bounded variation,

$$\int |K(x)| dx < \infty$$

$$K(x) \to 0 \text{ as } |x| \to \infty,$$

$$\int K(x) dx = 1,$$

$$\int |x \log|x||^{\frac{1}{2}} |dK(x)| < \infty,$$

and suppose f is uniformly continuous. Then if

$$h \to 0 \text{ as } n \to \infty$$

and

$$\frac{1}{nh} \log n \to 0 \text{ as } n \to \infty$$

$$\sup_R |\hat{f}(x) - f(x)| \to 0 \text{ almost surely as } n \to \infty.$$

Silverman (1978) also extends the results of Schuster (1969) and Van Ryzin (1969), establishing the exact rate of weak and strong uniform convergence of b $\{\hat{f}(x)\}$ to zero under mild conditions on h, f, and K.

Theorem 2.2.14: (Silverman, 1978). Let K satisfy the conditions of theorem 2.2.13 and let w, the modulus of continuity of K, satisfy

$$\int_0^1 (\log \frac{1}{u})^{\frac{1}{2}} \, d \, \{(w(u))^{\frac{1}{2}}\} < \infty.$$

Let f be uniformly continuous and as n → ∞ let

$$h \to 0, \quad \frac{1}{nh}(\log n)^2/\log(1/h) \to 0.$$

Then $(\frac{1}{nh} \log \frac{1}{h})^{-1} \sup_R \{\hat{f}(x) - E \{\hat{f}(x)\}\} \to C_1$ in probability, and $(\frac{1}{nh} \log \frac{1}{h})^{-1} \inf_R \{\hat{f}(x) - E \{\hat{f}(x)\}\} \to -C_1$ in probability where $C_1 = (2 \sup_R f(y) \int K^2(x)dx)^{\frac{1}{2}}$. If also $\Sigma h^\lambda < \infty$ for some λ then

$$1 <= C_1^{-1} \lim_{n \to \infty} \sup_R \{\frac{1}{nh} \log \frac{1}{h}\}^{-1} \sup_R |\hat{f}(x) - E \{\hat{f}(x)\} |$$

$$<= (1+\lambda)^{\frac{1}{2}} \text{ almost surely.}$$

Since this book is not primarily concerned with the estimation of probability density functions it would be inappropriate to pursue these matters any further here. Further results on convergence and consistency properties may be found in Van Ryzin (1966), Farrell (1972), Bickel and Rosenblatt (1973), Wahba (1975), Wagner (1975), Meyer (1977), Devroye and Wagner (1980) and many other papers. We will in fact present Van Ryzin's results in Section 2.3 when we study the multivariate case, and Wagner's results in Section 3.6 when we study variable (i.e. location dependent) kernel estimators.

Apart from consistency, there are other properties of the kernel estimator which are of interest (and relevance to us). For example, in view of the fact that the kernel estimate may be seen as an average of independent identically distributed elements it is hardly surprising to find that $\hat{f}(x)$ is asymptotically normally distributed.

<u>Theorem 2.2.15</u>: (Parzen, 1962). Let K(x) be a bounded density such that

$$\lim_{|x|\to\infty} xK(x) = 0$$

and let $h \to 0$, $nh \to \infty$ as $n \to \infty$. Then at every point x of continuity of f with $f(x) > 0$ $\hat{f}(x)$ is asymptotically normally distributed.

Just as the above theorems made use of (loose) constraints on the form of f in order to prove convergence results, the behaviour of the estimators can be improved if use can be made of any further properties which f is known to possess. For example, if f is known to be symmetric we can define the estimator

$$\hat{g}(x) = \tfrac{1}{2}\{\hat{f}(x) + \hat{f}(-x)\}.$$

For this estimator we have the following result:

<u>Theorem 2.2.16</u>: (Yamato, 1972). Let f(x) be symmetric about zero and let K(x) satisfy

$$K(x) = K(-x) \text{ for } x \in R$$

$$K(x) >= 0 \text{ for } x \in R$$

$$\int_R K(x)dx = 1$$

$$\lim_{n\to\infty}\int_{-\delta}^{\delta} K(x)dx = 1 \text{ for all } \delta > 0$$

$$\int_R K^2(x)dx < \infty$$

$K(x) \to 0$ uniformly as $n \to \infty$ on $(-\infty,-\delta)v(\delta,\infty)$ for all $\delta > 0$. Then

$$V\{\hat{g}(x)\} \quad <= V\{\hat{f}(x)\} \text{ for all x and n,}$$

$$\lim_{n\to\infty} nV\{\hat{g}(x)\}/\int_R K^2(x)dx = -f(x)/2$$

at all points of continuity of f, and

$$\lim_{n \to \infty} \frac{E\left|\hat{g}(x) - f(x)\right|^2}{E\left|\hat{f}(x) - f(x)\right|^2} \leq 1$$

at all non-zero points x of continuity of f.

The aim of this section has been to summarise some of the more fundamental and relevant theoretical results and give the reader an indication of the wealth of analytic knowledge which exists about kernel pdf estimators.

2.3   MULTIPLE CONTINUOUS VARIABLES

In the univariate case each design set point x_i contributed towards the estimate at x an amount inversely related to the distance between x and x_i. The nature of this inverse relationship was specified by the fundamental form of the kernel $K^*(x,x_i) = K(x-x_i)$ and by the smoothing parameter h. The multivariate extension of these univariate ideas is in principle straightforward. Again each design set point contributes to $\hat{f}(\underline{x})$ an amount which depends on the distance between $\underline{x}$ and $\underline{x}_i$. Again an average of these contributions is taken. Now, however, the K function has multiple arguments.

The general multivariate estimate is

$$\hat{f}(\underline{x}) = \frac{1}{n} \sum_{i=1}^{n} K^*(\underline{x},\underline{x}_i)$$

and we shall again focus on the case

$$\hat{f}(\underline{x}) = \frac{1}{n} \sum_{i=1}^{n} K(\underline{x}-\underline{x}_i). \tag{2.3.1}$$

Let us consider some special cases of K.

(i) $K(\underline{u}) = \dfrac{1}{(2\pi)^{d/2} \, |\underline{S}|^{\frac{1}{2}}} \exp\left\{-\tfrac{1}{2}\underline{u}'\underline{S}^{-1}\underline{u}\right\}$

The kernel centred at $\underline{x}_i$ has the same functional form as a d-dimensional multivariate normal distribution with mean $\underline{x}_i$. The advantages to be gained by taking K a probability density function, outlined in the preceding section, also apply here. There remains the question of choosing $\underline{S}$. Taken to an impracticable extreme, one could take a different $\underline{S}$ for each design set point (but see Section 3.6). More realistically, one could take a different $\underline{S}$ for each class. Many authors adopt this approach, though usually the form of $\underline{S}$ is constrained from the completely general matrix. (For example, Remme et al (1980) and many others use a diagonal matrix - see immediately below.) Shanmugam (1977), however, advocates the use of $\underline{S}$ proportional to the estimated covariance matrix of the class in question (obtained from the design set). He proves that the resulting density estimator is consistent. Van Ness (1980) considered this approach and rejected it on practical grounds because of the poor behaviour of the covariance matrix estimator with large numbers of variables.

$$\text{(ii)} \quad K(\underline{u}) = \frac{1}{h_1 \cdots h_d} \prod_{j=1}^{d} K_j(u_j/h_j)$$

For obvious reasons kernels of this form are termed product kernels. In one sense they are more general than (i) - they permit arbitrary marginal kernels, not constrained to be normal. The K_j can be any of the univariate forms to be discussed in Chapter 3. However, they are less general than (i) in the sense that they assume independence within the kernel (which does not imply that the estimate has independent variables, of course). A particular form of this K is derived from (i) by taking $\underline{S}$ to be diagonal.

(iii) $K(\underline{u}) = \dfrac{1}{h_1 \ldots h_d} \prod\limits_{j=1}^{d} K_1(u_j/h_j)$

Here we have taken $K_j \equiv K_1$ for $j = 2, \ldots, d$ in (ii). This is the most common form of product kernel for continuous variables. Indeed, when continuous variables alone are employed the present author has yet to see a mixture of kernel types used. However, when both continuous and categorical variables are used then (ii) is often applied (see Chapter 6).

(iv) $K(\underline{u}) = \dfrac{1}{h^d} \prod\limits_{j=1}^{d} K_1(u_j/h)$

Again this is a common form. It is simpler than (iii) in that only one parameter need be estimated. Superficially this is an important practical advantage but it might lead to seriously degraded performance. Consider, for example, estimating a bivariate normal distribution for which one variable has a variance of 0.1 and the other a variance of 100. A single h would tend to oversmooth the first variable and undersmooth the second. Some kind of standardisation seems to be called for. One way of tackling the problem which in effect uses a different h for each variable (and for each class) as in (iii) above and yet requires only a single parameter to be estimated for each class is as follows (see, for example Habbema and Hermans, 1977). If the smoothing parameter for class i and variable j is h_{ij}, then we let

$$h_{ij}^2 = c_i \, s_{ij}^2$$

where s_{ij}^2 is the sample variance for variable j and for class i. Now only c_i (i = 1, ..., c) must be estimated.

A theoretically oriented approach to finding multivariate kernels other than product kernels is presented in a very recent paper by Sacks and Ylvisaker (1981). We discuss this in Section 3.2. Apart from this, however, there appears to be very little work comparing the efficiency of these different multivariate kernels. We discuss choice of univariate kernels (and factors of product kernels) in Chapter 3, showing that most but not all of the evidence suggests that the form is relatively unimportant. Van Ness and Simpson (1976), for example, compared normal and Cauchy product kernels and obtained a negligible difference. On the other hand there is some slight evidence that the product form - which is the only multivariate form we have seen used in practical applications - may not always be ideal. Remme, Habbema and Hermans (1980), for example, carried out a Monte Carlo investigation on estimating correlated multivariate normal distributions using simple normal product kernels and showed that "some of the simulations with $d = 6$ and all correlations over 0.6 showed a more serious decrease of the performance of the kernel model."

Much of Section 2.2 can be extended immediately to the multivariate case. For example, Wertz (1978) quotes Vaduva (1963, 1968) as proving the following theorems, which are direct extensions of the Parzen (1962) asymptotic unbiasedness, pointwise consistency, and asymptotic normality results.

<u>Theorem 2.3.1</u>: If K is a bounded d-dimensional density with general dispersion parameter h_j in dimension j and

$$\lim_{||\underline{x}|| \to \infty} ||\underline{x}||^d \, |K(\underline{x})| = 0$$

and if $\lim_{n \to \infty} ||\underline{h}|| = 0$ then $\hat{f}(\underline{x})$ is asymptotically unbiased at every point of continuity of f.

<u>Theorem 2.3.2</u>: If in addition to the conditions on K and $\underline{h}$ in the preceding theorem we have

$$\lim_{n \to \infty} nh_1 \ldots \ldots h_d = \infty$$

then $\hat{f}(\underline{x})$ is pointwise consistent in the quadratic mean at every point of continuity of f.

<u>Theorem 2.3.3</u>: If in addition to the conditions on K and $\underline{h}$ in the preceding theorem we have

$$\int |K(\underline{x})|^{2+\delta} d\underline{x} < \infty \text{ for some } \delta > 0$$

$$\text{then } \lim_{n \to \infty} P \left\{ \frac{\hat{f}(\underline{x}) - E\{\hat{f}(\underline{x})\}}{V\{\hat{f}(\underline{x})\}} <= k \right\} = \frac{1}{\sqrt{2\pi}} \int_{-\infty}^{k} e^{-u^2/2} du$$

at points of continuity of f.

Cacoullos concentrates on the case of $h_j = h$ for $j = 1, \ldots, d$ and proves similar results. For example (c.f. theorem 2.2.11).

<u>Theorem 2.3.4</u>: (Cacoullos, 1966) If h satisfies

$$\lim_{n \to \infty} h = 0$$

$$\text{and } \lim_{n \to \infty} nh^{2d} = \infty$$

and if $k(u) = \int e^{iuy} K(y) dy$ is absolutely integrable for every $\delta > 0$

$$\lim_{n \to \infty} P \{\sup_{R^d} |\hat{f}(\underline{x}) - f(\underline{x})| > \delta\} = 0$$

And for the asymptotic form of the bias we have:

Theorem 2.3.5: (Cacoullos, 1966). If f has continuous partial derivatives of third order in a neighbourhood of $\underline{x}$ then $b(\underline{x}) = f(\underline{x}) - E\{\hat{f}(\underline{x})\}$ satisfies

$$\lim_{n \to \infty} b(\underline{x})/h^2 = -\tfrac{1}{2} \int \{\sum_{i=1}^{d} \sum_{j=1}^{d} \frac{\partial^2 f(x)}{\partial x_i \partial x_j} y_i y_j\} K(\underline{y}) d\underline{y}$$

(provided this integral converges absolutely).

Similarly, for product kernels of the form (ii), Epanechnikov (1969) establishes the following asymptotic results:

Theorem 2.3.6: (Epanechnikov, 1969). Let each K_j satisfy

$$0 \le K_j(x) < k < \infty$$

$$K_j(x) = K_j(-x)$$

$$\int K_j(x) dx = 1$$

$$\int x^2 K_j(x) dx = 1$$

$$\int x^m K_j(x) dx < \infty \text{ for } 0 \le m < \infty$$

and let $h_j \to 0$ as $n \to \infty$ and suppose that f has a Taylor expansion in all its arguments about each point $\underline{x}$. Then, as $n \to \infty$,

(i) $b(\underline{x}) \to -\tfrac{1}{2} \sum_{j=1}^{d} \partial^2 f(\underline{x})/\partial x_j^2 \; h_j^2.$

(ii) $MSE \to \frac{1}{n} f(\underline{x}) \prod_{j=1}^{d} \{\frac{1}{h_j} \int K_j^2(\underline{y}) d\underline{y}\} + \frac{1}{4} \{\sum_{j=1}^{d} \frac{\partial^2 f(x)}{\partial x_j^2} \cdot h_j^2\}$

(iii) $MISE \to \frac{1}{n} \sum_{j=1}^{d} \{\frac{1}{h_j} \int K_j^2(\underline{y}) d\underline{y}\} + \frac{1}{4} \int \{\sum_{j=1}^{d} \frac{\partial^2 f(x)}{dx_j^2} h_j^2\}^2 d\underline{x}$

Another form of consistency, and one which is particularly relevant to our problem of classification, has been introduced by Van Ryzin (1966). He defines a classification rule $D(\hat{f}_1, \hat{f}_2)$ as Bayes risk consistent if

$$P \{r(f,\hat{f}) >= \delta\} \to 0 \text{ as } n_1, n_2 \to \infty,$$

where $\quad r(f,\hat{f}) = R \{D(\hat{f}_1, \hat{f}_2)\} - R \{D(f_1,f_2)\}$

with R(G) the expected loss (risk) of the decision rule G and where $D(\hat{f}_1, \hat{f}_2)$ is the rule obtained by replacing the true densities f_1 and f_2 in the Bayes optimal rule $D(f_1,f_2)$ by kernel estimates $\hat{f}_1$ and $\hat{f}_2$. More generally, with $n_0 = \min(n_1,n_2)$, the rule $D(\hat{f}_1,\hat{f}_2)$ is said to be <u>Bayes risk consistent of order $\alpha(n_0)$</u> if

$$P \{q(n_0)r(f,\hat{f}) >= \delta\alpha(n_0)\} \to 0 \text{ as } n_0 \to \infty$$

where $q(n_0)$ is any sequence tending to zero as $n_0 \to \infty$.

Bayes risk consistency is seen to be directly concerned with the performance of the classifier, rather than of the density estimators. However, as we shall show below, the property of Bayes risk consistency can be derived from suitable properties of the estimators.

Van Ryzin demonstrates that the difference $r(f,\hat{f})$ for the risk of a classifier obtained by substituting estimates $\hat{f}_1$ and $\hat{f}_2$ for f_1 and f_2 in the Bayes optimum rule is bounded below and above by

$$0 <= r(f,\hat{f}) <= a_1\pi_1\int|\hat{f}_1(\underline{x})-f_1(\underline{x})|d\underline{x} + a_2\pi_2\int|\hat{f}_2(\underline{x})-f_2(\underline{x})|d\underline{x} \quad (2.3.2)$$

where a_i is the loss due to misclassifying a point from class $i(i=1,2)$ and there is no loss for a correct classification. He also shows that

$$P \{q(n_0)r(f,\hat{f}) >= \delta\alpha(n_0)\} <=$$

$$\frac{1}{\delta}q(n_0)\alpha(n_0)^{-1} \{\pi_1a_1\int E|\hat{f}_1(\underline{x})-f_1(\underline{x})|d\underline{x} +$$

$$\pi_2a_2\int E|\hat{f}_2(\underline{x})-f_2(\underline{x})|d\underline{x}\} \quad (2.3.3)$$

Using these inequalities Van Ryzin goes on to prove the following theorems:

<u>Theorem 2.3.7</u>: (Van Ryzin, 1966). Let $f_i(\underline{x})$ be continuous almost everywhere (i = 1,2). If $h \to 0$ as $n \to \infty$ and if $K(\underline{x})$ satisfies

$$\int K(\underline{x})d\underline{x} = 1$$

$$K(\underline{x}) >= 0$$

$$||\underline{x}||^d K(\underline{x}) \to 0 \text{ as } ||\underline{x}|| \to \infty$$

$$\sup_{R^d} K(\underline{x}) < \infty$$

then the decision rule $D(\hat{f}_1, \hat{f}_2)$ is Bayes risk consistent with $D(f_1, f_2)$.

<u>Theorem 2.3.8</u>:(Van Ryzin, 1966). Let f_1, f_2, h, and K be as in the preceding theorem and let h in addition satisfy

$$nh^d \to \infty \text{ as } n \to \infty,$$

and K in addition satisfy

$$\int ||\underline{x}|| K(\underline{x})d\underline{x} < \infty,$$

and let

$$E_i \left| \prod_{j=1}^{d} x_j \right|^{1+\delta} < \infty \text{ for some } \delta > 0 \qquad (2.3.4)$$

(E_i denoting expectation with respect to f_i, i = 1,2), and

$$\int |f_i(\underline{x}+\underline{y}) - f_i(\underline{x})| d\underline{x} < k_\alpha ||\underline{x}||^\alpha$$

for some $0 < \alpha <= 1$ and constant k_α. Then, choosing $h = 0 \ (n_i^{-1/(r+2\alpha)}$ implies that the decision rule $D(\hat{f}_1, \hat{f}_2)$ is Bayes risk consistent with $D(f_1,f_2)$ of order $n_0^{-\alpha/(r+2\alpha)}$.

Theorem 2.3.9: (Van Ryzin, 1966). Let $f_i(\underline{x})$ be continuous on R^d and let h and K satisfy the conditions of both of the preceding theorems. Assume also that (2.3.4) holds and that the following hold:

(i) $\int x_j K(\underline{x}) d\underline{x} = 0$ $j = 1,\ldots,d$

(ii) $f_i(\underline{x})$ has support set R^d, $i = 1,2$

(iii) $\partial^2 f_i / \partial x_j^2$ exists and is continuous on R^d, $i = 1,2$; $j = 1,\ldots,d$.

(iv) $\max_{i,j} \int\int \phi_{ij}(\underline{x},\underline{y}) d\underline{y}\ d\underline{x} < \infty$

where

$$\phi_{ij}(\underline{x},\underline{y}) = y_j^2 K(\underline{y}) \sup_{\theta \epsilon I_j} \frac{\partial^2 f_i}{\partial x_j^2}(x_1,\ldots,x_{j-1},\theta,x_{j+1},\ldots,x_d)$$

$$I_j = (x_j - |y_j|, x_j + |y_j|)$$

Then if $h = 0\ (n_i^{-1/(r+4)})$ the decision rule $D(\hat{f}_1,\hat{f}_2)$ is Bayes risk consistent of order $n_0^{-2/(r+4)}$.

Van Ryzin notes that the conditions of this last theorem are satisfied by the multivariate normal distribution. He also extends the results to unknown priors and to the multiclass case.

Glick (1972) has also examined convergence of classifiers based on kernel density estimators (and in fact generalised some of Van Ryzin's results). For example

Theorem 2.3.10: (Glick, 1972). If the estimates $\hat{f}_1,\ldots,\hat{f}_c$ are probability densities which converge pointwise (with probability one) to the true densities then (with probability one) the sample based non-error rate converges to the true non-error rate uniformly over the domain of all classification rules.

<u>Theorem 2.3.11</u>: (Glick, 1972). Subject to the conditions of the preceding theorem, the classification rule given by replacing the densities f_i in the optimum rule by estimates $\hat{f}_i$ is Bayes risk consistent. Moreover the apparent non-error rate is a consistent estimator of the optimum rate.

Devroye and Wagner (1980) have also generalised Van Ryzin's results. Finally, Greblicki (1978) also investigates the asymptotic optimality of classifiers based on pointwise consistent estimators such as the kernel method.

CHAPTER 3
Choice of Smoothing
Parameters and Kernel
for Continuous Variables

3.1   INTRODUCTION

It is well known that, at least as far as density estimation goes,
the choice of smoothing parameter h is critical. On the choice of K,
the kernel form, the bulk of the evidence to date suggests that it is
not so critical, but the evidence is not unanimous.   We elaborate on
this below.

The single class of measures of accuracy of estimate which has been
most widely studied as far as density estimation goes is based on mean
squared error. We open our discussion, in Section 3.2, with choices of
h and K based on minimising these mean squared error measures, before
we proceed to alternatives.   Some other measures in particular have
been adopted for use with kernel discriminant analysis (though they are
not necessarily ideally matched): most notable amongst these is the
cross-validation method based on the Kullback-Liebler loss, which is
set in context in Section 3.4.

Having outlined the methods, in Section 3.5 we consider more fundamental problems associated with choosing good h and K - and, indeed in choosing between methods for estimating them. Here we also summarise what experimental work exists.

The idea of using location dependent kernels was referred to briefly in Section 2.1. In Section 3.6 we develop this in detail, concentrating on the case of location dependent h. This general idea looks most promising and the author looks forward with interest to the results of future research on this method.

The whole area of choosing good h and K for use in kernel discriminant analysis has reached an interesting stage. Some very important results have been established but it is not yet clear which methods should be most popular for practical application. The next few years should see the established results being digested, their implications being understood and the gaps being filled in.

3.2   THE MSE AND MISE MEASURES

As will be evident from Section 2.2 there are two ways in which we may proceed, depending on whether density estimation is the means or the end. Although in our case it is merely a means, most of the theoretical work has taken estimation as the end, and we shall begin by outlining this. The difference depends on whether we restrict $K(x) >= 0$ or not - that is, whether we permit negative $\hat{f}(x)$. Note that although this distinction between the two approaches is useful from a practical viewpoint, from a theoretical viewpoint it is somewhat artificial. As will be clear from theorems 2.2.8 and 2.2.10, the $K(x) >= 0$ case is just a special case of the general situation of those theorems.

We began by assuming that K is an even bounded probability density function (pdf) such that

$$\int u^2 K(u)du < \infty.$$

Then, from (2.2.8) the asymptotic MSE is

$$\frac{f(x)}{nh} \int K^2(u)du + \frac{h^4}{4} f''(x)^2 (\int u^2 K(u)du)^2 \qquad (3.2.1)$$

(Note that $\int K^2(u)du < \infty$ by the conditions on K.)

Since K is a pdf we have $K(x) >= 0$ for all x and $K(x) \not\equiv 0$ so that

$$\int u^2 K(u)du > 0.$$

We can now modify K to make $\int u^2 K(u)du = 1$ without contravening any of the above restrictions on K. To see this let

$$\int u^2 K(u)du = 1/k^2$$

and define K*, the new kernel function, as

$$K^*(x) = \frac{1}{k} K(\frac{x}{k}).$$

Taking $k > 0$ leaves the evenness, boundedness, and non-negativity of K unaltered. Moreover

$$\int u^2 K^*(u)du = \int \frac{u^2}{k} K(\frac{u}{k})du.$$

Substituting $v = u/k$ gives

$$\int \frac{v^2 k^2}{k} K(v)k\ dv = k^2 \int v^2 K(v)dv = 1.$$

Similarly

$$\int K^*(u)du = \int \frac{1}{k} K(\frac{u}{k})du = \int \frac{1}{k} K(v)kdv = 1.$$

For simplicity of notation we write K instead of K*, K now satisfying

$$\int u^2 K(u)du = 1.$$

Having made this normalisation the asymptotic MSE (3.2.1) becomes

$$\frac{1}{nh} f(x) \int K^2(u)du + \frac{1}{4} \{f''(x)h^2\}^2,$$

and the asymptotic MISE (see also Section 2.2) becomes

$$\frac{1}{nh} \int K^2(u)du + \frac{1}{4} \int \{f''(x)h^2\}^2 dx. \qquad (3.2.2)$$

Differentiating this with respect to h and equating to zero yields

$$h_0 = \{\frac{\int K^2(u)du}{n\int f''(u)^2 du}\}^{1/5} \tag{3.2.3}$$

the asymptotically optimal h in the MISE sense. Note that the smoother is the pdf f, that is the smaller is $\int f''(u)^2 du$, the larger will be h_0 and the smaller will be the asymptotic MISE.

The optimal kernel shape can also be found from the asymptotic MISE. Epanechnikov (1969) uses calculus of variations and obtains, for K subject to the above constraints,

$$K_0(x) = \begin{cases} \dfrac{3}{4\sqrt{5}} - \dfrac{3x^2}{20\sqrt{5}} & |x| <= \sqrt{5} \\ \\ 0 & |x| > \sqrt{5} \end{cases} \tag{3.2.4}$$

Using both h_0 and K_0 the asymptotic MISE is

$$\frac{1}{4}(\frac{3}{n\sqrt{5}})^{4/5}(\int f''(u)^2 du)^{1/5} \tag{3.2.5}$$

This shows that for kernel estimators with $K(x) >= 0$ the rate of convergence of the MISE to zero is no better than $0(n^{-4/5})$. (Boyd and Steele (1978) generalise this to arbitrary estimators and show that there is no estimator which has a MISE convergence rate better than $0(n^{-1})$.)

If we substitute the MISE optimal h_0 (3.2.3) into the expression for the asymptotic MISE (3.2.2) we obtain

$$\frac{5}{4} \{\int K^2(u)du\}^{4/5} \{\int f''(u)^2 du\}^{1/5} n^{-4/5}$$

which permits us to compare the asymptotic MISE performance of any kernel K with that of the asymptotic MISE optimal kernel K_0 by studying the ratio.

$$T = \{\int K^2(u)du\}^{4/5}/\{\int K_0^2(u)du\}^{4/5}.$$

Examples of T for three common kernels are given in Table 3.1. (The

TABLE 3.1

Asymptotic ratios of MISE for kernel K to MISE for MISE optimal kernel
(3.2.4), both kernels using MISE optimal h.

K	I
$K(x) = \begin{cases} \frac{1}{2} & \|x\| \leqslant 1 \\ 0 & \|x\| > 1 \end{cases}$	1.65
$K(x) = \frac{1}{\sqrt{2}} e^{-x^2/2}$	1.04
$K(x) = \frac{1}{2} e^{-\sqrt{2}\|x\|}$	1.25

reader is cautioned about a number of arithmetic errors in the L column
of Epanechnikov (1969), Table 1.)

Although f is of course unknown, an idea of the best asymptotic MISE
we can hope to attain can be gained from Table 3.2. This shows the
value of the integral $(\int f''(u)du)^{1/5}$, which appears in the optimal
asymptotic MISE expression (3.2.5), for various choices of f.

Now let us return to the choice made at the beginning of this section
and relax the restriction $K(x) \geq 0$, acknowledging that to us pdf
estimation is not an end in itself and that the apparent disadvantage
of possibly obtaining $\hat{f}(x) < 0$ may not in fact be a disadvantage. In
Section 2.2 we showed (see theorems 2.2.6, 2.2.8, and 2.2.10) that the
bias and MISE of $\hat{f}$ could be reduced if we chose K from this more
general class.   In fact, a general expression for bias was given by
(2.2.7), namely

$$b\{\hat{f}(x)\} = -\sum_{r=1}^{m} \frac{h^r}{r!}f^{(r)}(x)\int_R u^r K(u)du + O\{h^{m+1}\} \qquad (3.2.6)$$

By imposing the conditions

$$\int x^r K(x)dx = 0. \quad \text{for } r = 1,\dots,m-1$$

$$\int |x^m K(x)|dx < \infty \qquad (3.2.7)$$

the bias becomes

$$b\{\hat{f}(x)\} = -\frac{h^m f^{(m)}(x)}{m!} \int u^m K(u)du + O\{h^{m+1}\} \quad . \qquad (3.2.8)$$

Moreover the optimal MSE of $\hat{f}(x)$ for K satisfying (3.2.7) tends to zero
as $n^{-2m/(2m+1)}$.   The common case of $K(x) \geq 0$ for all x occurs when
$m = 2$ in (3.2.7). If $m > 2$ is taken then the MSE convergence rate is
improved and we might also expect an improvement in small sample bias
resulting from the elimination of the extra terms in moving from
(3.2.6) to (3.2.8).

TABLE 3.2

Relative sizes of the asymptotically optimal MISE (3.2.5) for various
f.

f	$[\int f''(u)^2 du]^{1/5}$
$\dfrac{1}{\sqrt{2\pi}}\, e^{-x^2/2}$	0.733
$\dfrac{2}{\pi} \cdot \dfrac{1}{(1 + x)^2}$	1.955
$\dfrac{1}{\pi} \cdot \dfrac{1}{1 + x^2}$	0.842

The difficulty lies in finding a suitable K subject to the constraints of (3.2.7). Rather than confronting the problem by the head on approach of extending the m = 2 calculus of variations approach (see above and Epanechnikov, 1969), Schucany and Sommers (1977) cleverly approach the problem from the side and use a generalised jackknife method. This allows us to combine common m = 2 solutions to give overall K functions for which m > 2.

We shall illustrate with the simplest case of combining two simple m = 2 kernels. So, let

$$\hat{f}_{(1)}(x) = \frac{1}{nh_1} \sum_{i=1}^{n} K_1\left(\frac{x-x_i}{h_1}\right)$$

$$\hat{f}_{(2)}(x) = \frac{1}{nh_2} \sum_{i=1}^{n} K_2\left(\frac{y-y_i}{h_2}\right)$$

be two kernel estimates for the class in question, where K_1 and K_2 satisfy the constraints

$$\sup_{R} |K(x)| < \infty$$

$$\int K(x)dx = 1$$

$$\int |K(x)|dx < \infty$$

$$\int |x^m K(x)|dx < \infty \quad \text{(m an even integer)}$$

and let K_1 and K_2 be even functions. By virtue of this final property

$$\int u^r K(u)du = 0 \quad \text{for r odd,}$$

so that the terms in (3.2.6) with r odd disappear, leaving the bias

$$b\{\hat{f}(x)\} = -\sum_{s=1}^{t} \frac{f^{(2s)}(x)h^{2s} \int u^{2s}K(u)du}{(2s)!} + O\{h^{2t+1}\} \qquad (3.2.9)$$

where t = m/2.

Now define a new estimator

$$f^*(x) = \{\hat{f}_{(1)}(x) - R\hat{f}_{(2)}(x)\} \,/(1-R) \qquad (3.2.10)$$

with $R \neq 1$. From (3.2.9)

$$b\,\{f^*(x)\} = \frac{1}{1-R} \sum_{s=1}^{t} \{h_1^{2s}\int u^{2s}K_1(u)du - Rh_2^{2s}\int u^{2s}K_2(u)du\}.$$

$$\frac{f^{(2s)}(x)}{(2s)!} + 0\,\{h_1^{2t+1}\} + 0\,\{h_2^{2t+1}\} \qquad (3.2.11)$$

We can now eliminate the term with $s = 1$ - that is, the term in $f^{(2)}(x)$ - if we choose R such that

$$h_1^2 \int u^2 K_1(u)du - Rh_2^2 \int u^2K_2(u)du - 0.$$

Thus, referring to the original expression (3.2.6), we have eliminated all terms with odd r and the smallest term with even r.

From (3.2.10) we can see that $f^*(x)$ is in fact a kernel estimator with kernel

$$K_3(x) = \{K_1(x) - (Rh_1/h_2)K_2(x)\}/(1-R).$$

K_3 is a linear combination of K_1 and K_2.

We can in fact take this elimination of bias terms further. If we choose h_1 and h_2 in the ratio

$$h_1/h_2 = \{\frac{\int u^4 K_2(u)du \int u^2K_1(u)du}{\int u^4K_1(u)du \int u^2K_2(u)du}\}^{\frac{1}{2}}$$

it is easily seen that the term with $s = 2$ in (3.2.11), that is $r = 4$ in (3.2.6), is also eliminated - provided only that K_1 and K_2 differ in the second or fourth moments. Then, in terms of bias the expression (3.2.6) starts at sixth powers of h.

More general results, eliminating bias to still higher orders of h, can be obtained if more than two simple kernels are combined.

Schucany and Sommers (1977) give some comparative results of applying the conventional kernel estimate and their jackknifed estimate to estimating f(0) = 0.3989 in a standard normal distribution. Because these results are particularly interesting we reproduce them here as Table 3.3. Normal distributions were used both as the kernel of the conventional estimator and as the constituent components of the mixture kernel in the jackknifed estimator. $R = h_1^2/h_2^2$ was set to 0.99. For the conventional method h = 0.4267 is the asymptotically optimal h

$$h = \{\frac{f(x)}{n} \int K^2(u)du / \{f''(x) \int u^2 K(u)du\}\}^{1/5}$$

(see (3.2.3)) and h = 0.4502 is the h which minimises the MSE (n = 50). Apart from the fact that the jackknifed estimator gives smaller MSE's than the conventional approach, the reciprocal relationship between the bias and variance of f* is worthy of note. Thus a bias comparable in size to that of $\hat{f}$ (occurring when h is large) is accompanied by a substantially smaller variance and vice versa.

Schucany and Sommers (1977) present further results for other x values with f normal and also for f exponential and with a uniform kernel. The superior MSE performance of the jackknifed estimator is evident in most cases, though not always. Schucany and Sommers observe that some "caution must also be exercised in selecting h_1 and h_2".

If we focus our attention on the choice of h which minimises the MISE of $\hat{f}$ based on these more general kernels (see theorem 2.2.10) then we easily find the optimal h. For example, Wertz (1970) gives

TABLE 3.3

Comparison of conventional kernel estimator ($\hat{f}$) and the jackknifed estimator (f^*) of Schucany and Sommers (1977) on estimating $f(0)$ in a standard normal distributions.

Estimator	h_1	Bias	Variance	MSE
$\hat{f}$	.4267	.0320	.002357	.003381
$\hat{f}$	.4502	.0351	.002117	.003354
f^*	.65	.0149	.002568	.002790
f^*	.70	.0185	.002187	.002530
f^*	.75	.0225	.001867	.002375
f^*	.80	.0268	.001601	.002315
f^*	.90	.0362	.001180	.002496

56

Theorem 3.2.1: Under the conditions of theorem 2.2.10 if h is of the form $kn^{-\alpha}$ the order of convergence of the MISE is $n^{-2m/(2m+1)}$ and is achieved when

$$\alpha = (2m + 1)^{-1}$$

$$k = \{\frac{2m\{\int u^m K(u)du\}^2 \int f^{(m)}(u)^2 du}{(m!)^2 \int K^2(u)du}\}^{-1/(2m+1)}$$

Woodroofe (1970) proposes an iterative procedure for estimating h. He begins with an arbitrary $h^{(1)}$ and uses this to yield estimate $\hat{f}_{(1)}(x)$. This is used in place of f(x) in the expression for asymptotic MSE. (Our expression (3.2.1) although in fact Woodroofe, in his Corollary 2.2, uses a more general expression corresponding to m > 2 in theorems 2.2.8 and 2.2.10 and in the above discussion.) This yields a new estimate for h, say $h^{(2)}$. Finally, $h^{(2)}$ yields $\hat{f}_{(2)}(x)$. Woodroofe proves that

$$E\{\hat{f}_{(2)}(x) - f(x)\}^2/E\{\hat{f}_{(0)}(x) - f(x)\}^2 \to 0 \text{ as } n \to \infty$$

where $\hat{f}_{(0)}(x)$ signifies the estimate with the optimal h.

Sacks and Ylvisaker (1981) have also studied kernels which asymptotically minimise the MSE at a point (which, without loss of generality, they take to be 0). The reader will have noticed that our discussion so far has concentrated on the univariate case. This reflects both the emphasis in the literature and the ubiquity of product kernels in multivariate cases. However, the product kernel is, as we pointed out in Section 2.3, not the only multivariate generalisation. Sacks and Ylvisaker present a more general extension to d > 1 and also consider the case when $\underline{x}$ lies at a boundary of the support set of f. Cases involving the latter could occur if, for example, on some variable all scores greater than X have been set equal to X (saturation of a measuring instrument. Truncation of all ages to two year digits in a computer coding of a questionnaire). This could

be important in high dimensional spaces when the volume at the boundary

becomes far greater than the volume near the centre (due to the curse

of dimensionality). So that we can express the results in the form

Sacks and Ylvisaker give them we work with G instead of K where

$$K(\underline{x}) = \rho^{2d/(2k+d)} G(\rho^{2/(2k+d)} \underline{x})$$

where $\rho = \sqrt{(m^2 n/(\alpha+\delta))}$ with $\delta > 0$, $\alpha = f(\underline{0})$, and m a fixed positive

number such that

$$|r(\underline{x})| \leq m||\underline{x}||^k$$

for $\underline{x} \in S_0 = \{\underline{x}| \ ||\underline{x}|| \leq s_0\}$, a fixed sphere about 0 and where k and

r(x) are given by

$$f(\underline{x}) = \alpha + \sum_{1\leq\Sigma(\underline{j})\leq k-1} \frac{\partial^{j1}...\partial^{jd}}{\partial x_1^{j1}...\partial d_d^{jd}} (f(\underline{0})) \frac{x_1^{j1}...x_d^{jd}}{j_1!...j_d!} + r(\underline{x})$$

for $\underline{x} \in R^d$. (Here $\Sigma(\underline{j}) = j_1 +...+ j_d$). On choosing m, Sacks and

Ylvisaker say: "some scant information obtained in regression contexts

indicates that crude methods may be adequate since the estimate $\hat{f}(\underline{0})$

seems to be insensitive to misspecification of m." The asymptotically

MSE optimal kernel is then given by

$$G(\underline{x}) = \{\Sigma_{\underline{j}}(c_{\underline{j}}x_1^{j1}...x_d^{jd}) - \theta||\underline{x}||^k\}_+$$

$$- \{\Sigma_{\underline{j}}(c_{\underline{j}} x_1^{j1}...x_d^{jd}) + \theta||\underline{x}||^k\}_- \qquad (3.2.12)$$

where $c_{\underline{j}}$ and θ are obtained by constraints on the kernel form. The

subscripts + and - mean that, in the first case the function is

truncated to be non-negative, and in the second case to be

non-positive. Table 3.4 reproduces (with permission) Table 1 of Sacks and Ylvisaker, showing optimal G for different degrees and intervals. The column headed "interval" refers to different cases of S_0 above and G_+ is

$$G_+ = \sum_{\underline{j}} (c_{\underline{j}} \; x_1^{j1}\ldots x_d^{jd}) - \theta ||\underline{x}||^k. \qquad (3.2.13)$$

The fourth line in this table corresponds to the Epanechnikov kernel. Note the last two lines, which give fundamental generalisations of the MSE approach to d > 1. Sacks and Ylvisaker compare the relative efficiency of product kernels using Epanechnikov and Rosenblatt components with the more fundamental generalisation given in the last line. The relative efficiencies of these two product kernels is given in Table 3.5. (Reproduced with permission) Sacks and Ylvisaker remark that the performance of standard kernels is not much worse than that of the optimal ones when $\underline{0}$, the point at which they are obtaining the estimate, is an interior point of the support set of f. However, when $\underline{0}$ is at or near an end point the standard kernels introduce a large bias term and the Sacks and Ylvisaker kernels are to be preferred.

These results are all very well but we must always bear in mind that they are derived from asymptotic arguments and might be of limited value unless n is large. In the remainder of this section we summarise the work on small samples.

Scott, Tapia and Thompson (1977) (see also Scott and Factor, 1981) have extended Woodroofe's suggestion of iteration and presented small sample simulation results. As before we have the asymptotic MISE optimal h given by

$$\hat{h} = \{\int K^2(u)du\}^{1/5} \; \{\int u^2 K(u)du\}^{-2/5} \; \{\int f''(u)^2 du\}^{-1/5} n^{-1/5} \qquad (3.2.14)$$

Scott et al use a normal kernel, so that in this expression only

TABLE 3.4

Examples of asymptotically mean square efficient kernels for different dimensionalities (d) and degrees (k). (Sacks and Ylvisaker, 1981).

d	k	Interval	G_+ (see (3.2.13))
1	1	$(-\infty,\infty)$ or $[-\xi,\infty), \xi \geqslant 3^{1/3}$	$.693 - .481\,\lvert x\rvert$
1	1	$[0,\infty)$	$1.11 - 6.06\,\lvert x\rvert$
1	1	$[-\xi,\infty), \xi < 3^{1/3}$	(*1)
1	2	$(-\infty,\infty)$	$.576 - .339\,x^2$
1	2	$[0,\infty)$	$2.81 - 3.01\,x - .75\,x^2$
1	2	$[-.5,\infty)$	$.902 - .766\,x - .159\,x^2$
1	2	$[-1,\infty)$	$.586 - .056\,x - .308\,x^2$
1	3	$(-\infty,\infty)$	$.901 - .945^2 x - .359\,\lvert x\rvert^3$
1	4	$(-\infty,\infty)$	$.96 - 1.2\,x^2 - .33\,x^4$
d	1	R^d	$\dfrac{(v_1-v_2)^{d/(d+2)}}{(v_0-v_1)}\,[1 - (v_1-v_2)^{1/(d+2)}\lvert\lvert \underline{x}\rvert\rvert]$ (*2)
d	2	R^d	$\dfrac{(v_2-v_4)^{d/(d+4)}}{(v_0-v_2)}\,[1 - (v_2-v_4)^{2/(d+4)}\lvert\lvert \underline{x}\rvert\rvert^2]$ (*2)

(*1) For $0 < \xi < 3^{1/3}$ solve $\int_{-\xi}^{\infty} (c_0 - \theta\lvert x\rvert)_+ dx = \theta$ and obtain c_0/θ as the real root of $u^3 + 3u\xi^2 - 2\xi^3 - 6 = 0$. Then $\int_{-\xi}^{c_0} [c_0/\theta - \lvert u\rvert] du = 1/\theta$ determines θ.

(*2) $v_j = \int_{\lvert\lvert \underline{x}\rvert\rvert \leqslant 1} \lvert\lvert \underline{x}\rvert\rvert^j \, d\underline{x} = \dfrac{d}{j+d}\, v_0$.

$v_0 = \dfrac{\pi^{d/2}}{(d/2)!}$ if d is even.

$v_0 = \pi^{(d-1)/2}\, 2^d\, (\tfrac{d-1}{2})!/d!$ if d is odd.

TABLE 3.5

Asymptotic relative efficiency of Epanechnikov product kernels and
Rosenblatt product kernels compared to the second degree d > 1
asymptotic MSE optimal kernel (Sacks and Ylvisaker, 1981).

d	Epanechnikov	Rosenblatt
1	1	.94
2	.99	.89
4	.95	.83
8	.91	.75
∞	.67	.49

$$\beta(f) = \{\int f''(u)^2 du\}^{-1/5} \qquad (3.2.15)$$

remains undetermined. A little algebra then shows that if $f''(x)$ is replaced by $\hat{f}^{(i)}{}''(x)$, with the estimate based on $h = h_i$, we have

$$\beta(\hat{f}^{(i)})^{-5} = \frac{3}{8\sqrt{\pi}n^2 h_i^9} \sum_{j=1}^{n} \sum_{k=1}^{n} \{h^4 - (x_j - x_k)^2 h_i^2 +$$

$$\frac{1}{12}(x_j - x_k)^4\} \exp \{-(x_j - x_k)^2/4h_i^2\}.$$

Substituting this back into (3.2.15) and (3.2.14) leads to an iterative procedure for h, namely

$$h_{i+1} = \{\int K^2(u)du\}^{1/5} \{\int u^2 K(u)du\}^{-2/5} \{\int \hat{f}^{(i)}{}''(x)^2 dx\}^{-1/5} n^{-1/5}$$

The authors choose the largest non-negative solution of this iterative procedure as their estimate. (Choosing the starting value h_0 = (sample range) guarantees convergence to the largest solution).

Anderson (1969) has made a detailed comparison of kernel and orthogonal series estimators and during the course of this he presented MISE optimal values of h for various distributions, kernels and sample sizes. Figure 3.1 shows some of these results when the standard normal density is being estimated using normal, double exponential and uniform kernels. Figure 3.1(a) shows the optimal h and 3.1(b) the corresponding MISE values. For curves A, B, and C the optimal h is chosen by numerical minimisation of the MISE function. For D h is given by the Rosenblatt (1956) approximation to the optimal h. (This assumes an h of the form $cn^{-1/5}$ and finds $c = (12\sqrt{2})^{1/5}$ by truncating the expansion of the MSE). Note that

$$\text{MISE} \{\hat{f}(h), f(\sigma)\} = k\text{MISE}\{\hat{f}(kh), f(k\sigma)\} \qquad (3.2.16)$$

62

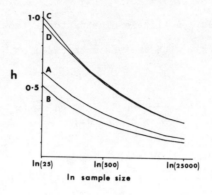

(a)

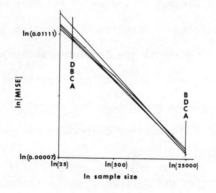

(b)

Figure 3.1 (a) Optimal h and (b) resulting MISE when estimating the standard normal density using different kernels. A: normal kernel. B: double exponential kernel. C: uniform kernel. D: uniform kernel using Rosenblatt h.

where we have temporarily adopted the notation of letting the arguments of $\hat{f}$ and f be, respectively, the smoothing parameter of the kernel estimator and the standard deviation of f. Thus, in particular, if $\hat{h}$ is the h which minimises $\text{MISE}\{\hat{f}(h), f(\sigma)\}$ then $k\hat{h}$ is the h which minimises $\text{MISE}\{\hat{f}(h), f(k\sigma)\}$. This means that the results in Figure 3.1 are easily generalised. It also follows from (3.2.16) that the estimates become better in terms of MISE as the variance of the pdf being estimated increases. As Anderson concludes, and as is evident from Figure 3.1, "although the accuracy of the density estimate, as measured by (the optimal) MISE, may not be appreciably influenced by the choice of kernel, the choice of optimal h can be extremely different for different kernels."

Anderson (1969) has also given extensive analytic derivations of the minimum MISE associated with estimating different densities using normal kernels. Figures 3.2(a) and (b) show, respectively, the minimising h and the minimum MISE when an exponential density with variance 1 and a uniform density with variance 1 are being estimated from samples of different sizes. The differences between these results and those of curve A of Figure 3.1 are worth noting. Certainly the asymmetry of the exponential distribution, as contrasted with the symmetry of the normal distribution seems to lead to a large difference in the optimal h. (However, on the subject of asymmetric f's see also Section 3.6 on location dependent spread parameters.) Note also that an incorrect assumption about distributional form could have major consequences in terms of MISE accuracy. Suppose, for example, that we had a sample of $n = 1000$ observations from a uniform distribution which we incorrectly assumed was normal. From Figure 3.1 the optimal h is

64

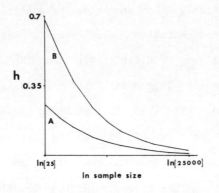

(a)

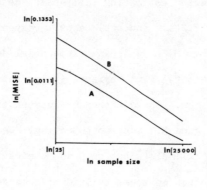

(b)

Figure 3.2 (a) Optimal h and (b) resulting MISE
when estimating (A) the exponential and (B) the
uniform densities with variance 1 using normal
kernels.

0.2723 with an associated MISE of 0.0010. In fact, however, we see from Figure 3.2 that this h will lead to a MISE of over 0.0081, greater by a factor of 8. The best h for the uniform distribution would be h = 0.1200, only half the chosen size. One way to ease the problem might be to transform the data (to, say, normality) prior to estimating the density, and then retransforming back (but see Section 3.6).

Fryer (1976) has also studied MSE and related measures for use in estimating h. It seems more appropriate, however, to present his results in Section 3.5, where we consider the sensitivity of various measures of performance to the chosen value of h.

Watson and Leadbetter (1963) have used analytic techniques to find the optimal K for finite n by minimising the MISE. The minimum MISE may be expressed as

$$\frac{1}{2\pi} \int_{-\infty}^{\infty} \frac{|\phi_f(t)|^2 \{1-|\phi_f(t)|^2\}}{1 + (n-1)|\phi_f(t)|^2} \, dt$$

where $\phi_f(t)$ is the Fourier transform of $f(x)$. This minimum is achieved when

$$K(x) = \frac{1}{2\pi} \int_{-\infty}^{\infty} e^{-itx} \frac{|\phi_f(t)|^2}{\frac{1}{n} + \frac{n-1}{n}|\phi_f(t)|^2} \, dt$$

We give below some examples of particular pdf's $f(x)$ and their associated MISE minimising kernel functions, $K_0(x)$:

(i) $f(x) = 1/\pi(1+x^2)$ (Watson and Leadbetter, 1963)

$$K_0(x) = \frac{n}{n-1} \cdot \frac{e^{-\pi x/2}}{1-e^{-\pi x}} \sin \frac{x \log(n-1)}{2} + \frac{2n}{\pi} \sum_{i=1}^{\infty} (\frac{-1}{n-1})^{r+1} \frac{r}{x^2+4r^2}$$

(ii) $f(x) = x^{p-1} e^{-x}/\Gamma(p)$, p a positive integer. (Watson and Leadbetter, 1963).

$$K_0(x) = \frac{n^{3/4}}{2(n-1)^{\frac{1}{2}}} \exp\{-xn^{1/4}\sin\frac{\alpha}{2}\} \cos\{|x|n^{1/4}\cos\frac{\alpha}{2} - \frac{\alpha}{2}\}$$

where

$$\alpha = \pi - \tan^{-1}\{(n-1)^{\frac{1}{2}}\}.$$

(iii) $f(x) = \dfrac{1}{\sigma\sqrt{2\pi}} \exp\{-(x-\mu)^2/2\sigma^2\}$ (Wertz, 1978).

$$K_0(x) = \frac{1}{h\sqrt{2\pi}} \exp\{-x^2/2h^2\}$$

(iv) $f(x) = \quad 1$ if $|x| < \frac{1}{2}$ (Wertz, 1978)

              0 otherwise

$$K_0(x) = \quad \frac{1}{h} \text{ if } |x| < \frac{1}{2}$$

              0 otherwise.

Of course these results are of more theoretical than practical value because, although one might be prepared to assume that f takes one of the above forms, in general f will be unknown.

We commented in Section 2.2 that convergence of $\hat{f}$ to f in senses other than MSE and MISE has also been studied. Exactly the same applies here - criteria other than MSE and MISE have also been used to assess the performance of kernel estimators and to estimate the smoothing parameters and kernel shapes. We discuss some of these in the next section.

3.3   OTHER MEASURES

In a perfectly general sense one can regard estimation as being the process of optimising a prespecified objective function by choice of the parameters (or whatever) to be estimated. Different objective functions will lead to different estimates. Thus care should be taken to ensure that the chosen objective function - and hence the chosen estimator - possesses properties which are regarded as desirable. Naturally, what is desirable in one context may not be so in another. A simple example of this situation is found in the use of several different estimates of location - whether the mean, median, or mode should be used depends on what one is trying to do. In the preceding section we discussed the use of the MSE and MISE as objective functions from which to derive estimates of h and k. But other functions - other measures of the difference between $\hat{f}$ and f - have been used, and in some circumstances (with some aims in mind) their properties may be regarded as more desirable than those of MSE or MISE.

An example of an alternative criterion being used to derive a suitable K is given by Boneva, Kendall and Stefanov (1971). Rather than starting from a definition of their objective function, however, it is more convenient to begin by showing how their estimate is defined. Instead of forming a smooth pdf estimate from a raw empirical distribution they begin with a histogram and seek to smooth this, so let $\underline{\phi}$ be a vector whose ith component is the number of points falling in the ith cell of the histogram. We can generalise this by letting the ϕ_i be non-integral and requiring $\Sigma\phi_i^2 < \infty$. Let Φ be the space of such generalised histograms. Then, through some rather elegant functional analysis, Boneva et al establish a space, S, the elements of which can be mapped one-to-one to the elements of Φ by the mapping

$$\theta s = \underline{\phi}; \ s \ \epsilon \ S, \underline{\phi} \ \epsilon \ \Phi$$

with ϕ_i being the integral under s over the ith histogram cell. S consists of exactly those continuous and continuously differentiable functions which are such that

(a) in each cell of the grid s(x) is a quadratic function of x,

(b) $\int_{-\infty}^{\infty} s^2(x)dx < \infty$.

From this, by considering the special case of a single observation and making use of the relation between S and Φ, Boneva et al go on to derive the unit histospline or deltaspline. This is the fundamental building block of their estimate and serves the same role as our kernel function. Three constraints (cell volume and continuity conditions between neighbouring cells) impose conditions permitting the coefficients in the quadratic in each cell to be determined. Table 3.6 from Boneva et al (reproduced with permission), gives these coefficients.

From here Boneva et al go on to generalise their estimator by relaxing the histogram cell structure and instead positioning one deltaspline kernel function at each of the raw data points. This is thus the usual form of kernel estimator.

Let us now return to consider what objective function is implicitly used in this estimator. In deriving the estimator Boneva et al begin with a large class, T, of smooth functions (the details are unnecessary here and may be found in the reference) and restrict it to the domain S defined above by requiring s ϵ S to satisfy

(i) $\int_{-\infty}^{\infty} s'(x)z'(x)dx = 0$

for all z ϵ Z where Z is the set of t ϵ T such that $\theta t = \underline{0}$,

(ii)   for a given $\underline{\phi}$ ϵ Φ, t = s is the unique solution to $\theta t = \underline{\phi}$ which minimises

$$\int_{-\infty}^{\infty} \sigma'(x)^2 dx.$$

Thus instead of minimising the MISE, the Boneva et al estimator

TABLE 3.6

Coefficients for the deltaspline of Boneva et al (1971). Cell number 7 is the "occupied" cell.

Cell	Constant	Coefficient of x	Coefficient of x^2
1	2.3463×10^{-4}	8.1278×10^{-4}	-1.9230×10^{-3}
2	-8.7565×10^{-4}	-3.0333×10^{-3}	7.1770×10^{-3}
3	3.2679×10^{-3}	1.1320×10^{-2}	-2.6785×10^{-2}
4	-1.2196×10^{-2}	-4.2249×10^{-2}	9.9962×10^{-2}
5	4.5517×10^{-2}	1.5767×10^{-1}	-3.7306×10^{-1}
6	-1.6987×10^{-1}	-5.8845×10^{-1}	1.3923
7	6.3397×10^{-1}	2.1961	-2.1961
8	6.3397×10^{-1}	-2.1961	1.3923
9	-1.6987×10^{-1}	5.8845×10^{-1}	-3.7306×10^{-1}
10	4.5517×10^{-2}	-1.5767×10^{-1}	9.9962×10^{-2}
11	-1.2196×10^{-2}	4.2249×10^{-2}	-2.6785×10^{-2}
12	3.2679×10^{-3}	-1.1320×10^{-2}	7.1770×10^{-3}
13	-8.7565×10^{-4}	3.0333×10^{-3}	-1.9230×10^{-3}

minimises a "smoothness" objective function.

Silverman (1978a) has applied criteria of uniform difference between $\hat{f}$ and f to the problem of selecting h in the univariate case. In fact the method can be extended to the multivariate case but practical difficulties are encountered. Silverman focusses his attention on h rather than K, noting that the choice of the former is more critical than the latter, and uses as kernel

$$K(x) = \begin{cases} \dfrac{x^4}{4} - \dfrac{|x|^3}{2} + \dfrac{1}{2} & \text{for } |x| <= 1 \\[2mm] \dfrac{|x|}{4}(2-|x|)^3 & \text{for } 1 <= |x| <= 2 \\[2mm] 0 & \text{for } |x| >= 2 \end{cases}$$

This is similar to Epanechnikov's (1969) (3.2.4) asymptotically MISE optimal kernel, it has a bounded region of support, and is a piecewise polynomial, both of which properties lead to easy computation. It also satisfies the analytic conditions (a) to (h) below. Silverman's method for choosing h is based on the following theorem.

Theorem 3.3.1: (Silverman, 1978a) Suppose that the true real density f has a uniformly continuous second derivative and that the kernel K satisfies

(a) K has a uniformly continuous second derivative of bounded variation.

(b) $K^{(j)}(x) \to 0$ as $x \to \infty$ for $j = 0,1,2$

(c) $\int |K^{(j)}(x)| dx < \infty$ for $j = 0,1,2$; $\int K(x)dx = 1$.

(d) $\int_0^1 (\log^1/u)^{\frac{1}{2}} d\gamma_j(u) < \infty$ for $j = 0$ and 2, where γ_j is the positive square root of the modulus of continuity of $K^{(j)}$.

(e) $\int |x\log|x||^{\frac{1}{2}} |K'(x)| dx < \infty$

(f) The Fourier transform of K is not identically zero in any neighbourhood of zero.

(g) $\int x K(x) dx = 0.$

(h) $\int x^2 K(x) dx \neq 0.$

Choose $h = h(n)$ to give the best possible rate of uniform convergence of $\hat{\delta}f$ as $n \to \infty$. Then

$$\sup \{\hat{f}'' - E \{\hat{f}''\}\} \to k \sup|f''|$$

$$\inf \{\hat{f}'' - E \{\hat{f}''\}\} \to -k \sup|f''|$$

in probability as $n \to \infty$. For the above kernel $k \simeq 0.4$.

This means that if h^* is the best choice of h then the random fluctuations in $\hat{f}''$ will be asymptotically of maximum size $\pm k \sup|f''|$.

In graphs of $\hat{f}''$ for various h's the systematic variation gives an estimate of f'' - and hence of $\sup|f''|$. That particular $h = h^*$ should be chosen which gives fluctuations of height about $\pm 0.4 \sup|f''|$ about the systematic variation. Thus "the ideal test graph (i.e. graph of $\hat{f}''$) should have fluctuations which are quite marked but do not obscure the systematic variation completely." Silverman gives illustrations of this method applied to real data. While the method is subjective the examples are sufficiently illuminating for one to expect similar results from different analysts. However, although the method seeks to identify that h which gives the best possible rate of uniform convergence it remains to be seen whether it performs better than simple subjective evaluation of systematic versus random variation in univariate plots of $\hat{f}$. Moreover, the difficulty of extending it to $d > 2$ means that it is of limited value for our application - although obviously an h could be chosen for each marginal separately, as with the other methods.

Breiman, Meisel and Purcell (1977) have presented a quite different criterion. Let b_j represent the distance between point $\underline{x}_j$ and its nearest neighbour in the design set (for this class) and let $V(r)$ be the volume of a d-dimensional hypersphere of radius r. So

$$V(r) = \pi^{d/2} r^d / \Gamma(d/2 + 1).$$

Then the random variables w_j, defined by

$$w_j = \exp\{-nf(\underline{x}_j)V(b_j)\} \quad j = 1,\ldots,n$$

have an approximately uniform univariate distribution. Thus if we replace $f(\underline{x}_j)$ by the estimate $\hat{f}(\underline{x}_j)$ we have an estimate, $\hat{w}_j$, for w_j and we can measure how much the $\hat{f}$ differs from f by seeing how much the distribution of the $\hat{w}_j$ differs from the uniform distribution. A suitable criterion is thus

$$\sum_{j=1}^{n} \{w_{(j)} - j/n\}^2 \tag{3.3.1}$$

where $\hat{w}_{(j)}$ is the jth ordered w_i.

The above criteria suggested by Boneva et al, Silverman and Breiman et al are perhaps not the most obvious measures of difference between f and $\hat{f}$ and others can easily be invented. For example, in assessing the performance of their estimators (as distinct from the use as criteria on which the estimates are based) Breiman et al use the following three measures:

(i)
$$\frac{1}{n\hat{\sigma}_f^2} \sum_{i=1}^{n} \{f(x_i) - \hat{f}(x_i)\}^2 \tag{3.3.2}$$

where
$$\hat{\sigma}_f^2 = \frac{1}{n} \sum_{i=1}^{n} \{f(x_i) - \hat{\mu}_f\}^2$$

and
$$\hat{\mu}_f = \frac{1}{n} \sum_{i=1}^{n} f(x_i)$$

(ii)
$$\frac{1}{n\hat{\mu}_f} \sum_{i=1}^{n} |f(x_i) - \hat{f}(x_i)| \tag{3.3.3}$$

(iii) $\frac{1}{n} \sum\limits_{i=1}^{n} |f(x_i) - \hat{f}(x_i)|/f(x_i)$ (3.3.4)

Raatgever and Duin (1978) note that (i)-(iii) only measure the difference at the design set points and they also use the Kolmogorov variational distance, defined by

$$1 - \int \min \{f(x), \hat{f}(x)\} dx \qquad (3.3.5)$$

This, like the MISE, compares f and $\hat{f}$ at all x's. The Kolmogorov measure, in the more general pattern recognition context, is more usually applied to measuring the separability between two classes - as for example in variable selection. This immediately suggests that other measures, perhaps normally seen as inter-class separability measures, could be applied in our context. De Figueiredo (1974) considers integrated squared error analogous to (i). In fact he represents the kernel function as a truncated expansion of basis functions and estimates the coefficients.

At the beginning of this section we noted that different measures reflected different aspects of the similarity between f and $\hat{f}$ and that a measure could be chosen which reflected those aspects of particular relevance for the purpose at hand. For the purposes of classification Breiman et al suggest that, of the measures (i)-(iii) above, (iii) may be the most appropriate. One can take this idea further. Let us denote a general measure of the difference between f and $\hat{f}$ at x by $D\{f(x), \hat{f}(x)\}$. Moreover, for simplicity let us consider only the two class case, denoting the true pdf of class i by f_i and its estimate by $\hat{f}_i (i = 1, 2)$. Then we can define a general measure

$$\int \{|D\{f_1(x), \hat{f}_1(x)\}| + |D\{f_2(x), \hat{f}_2(x)\}|\} \cdot w\{f_1(x), f_2(x)\} dx \qquad (3.3.6)$$

where $w(a,b)$ is a weight function which decreases monotonically with increasing distance between a and b. Thus when $f_1(x)$ and $f_2(x)$ are close w is large and there is a premium on making $\left|D\{f_1(x),\hat{f}_1(x)\}\right|$ and $\left|D\{f_2(x),\hat{f}_2(x)\}\right|$ small – that is, on making $\hat{f}_i(x) \simeq f_i(x)$, i = 1,2, near the decision surface.

One criterion which is obviously relevant is the straightforward misclassification rate. Dubuisson and Lavison (1980) have applied the kernel method in detecting abnormal states of a nuclear reactor and during their investigation they compared several different kernel shapes using error rate. Their problem had two classes, with a design set of 64 from each class and a test set of 64 from each class. There were 16 variables. They used product kernels with identical factors, these being chosen from those in Table 3.7. The smoothing parameter was estimated by two methods: (i) Using (3.2.3) with f assumed normal, (ii) h = $n^{-1/4d}$. The estimated error rates are shown in Table 3.7. It is interesting and curious that the exponential kernel should be so much better than the other methods. This study is one of very few which suggest that the choice of the factors in K might be so important. It seems likely that the contradiction between this and other studies (e.g. Van Ness and Simpson, 1976) is due to an unfortunately good match of the kernel to the synthetic data in Monte Carlo comparisons. It would be interesting to look closely at the Dubuisson and Lavison data to see if a transformation (as suggested by Ojo, 1974, and Fryer, 1977) might not substantially improve the performance with normal kernels.

As a final criterion we introduce a measure which in one form or another has played (and continues to play) a very important role in kernel estimation. We shall discuss this measure and its importance at some length in the next section (and in Chapter 4) and so content

TABLE 3.7

Error rates in the Dubuisson and Lavison (1980) study for different kernel shapes.

Kernel	h method (i)	h method (ii)
$\frac{3}{4\sqrt{5}}$ $(1 - \frac{x^2}{5})$ for $|x| \leq \sqrt{5}$ 0 $\quad$ for $|x| > \sqrt{5}$ (see 3.2.4)	.43	.43
$\frac{\alpha}{4} \cos \frac{\alpha x}{4}$ for $|x| \leq \frac{\pi}{\alpha}$ 0 $\quad$ for $|x| > \frac{\pi}{\alpha}$ $(\alpha = \sqrt{\pi^2 - 8})$	.50	.47
$\frac{1}{\sqrt{6}} - \frac{|x|}{6}$ for $|x| \leq \sqrt{6}$ 0 $\quad$ for $|x| > \sqrt{6}$	.30	.30
$e^{-x^2/2}/\sqrt{2\pi}$. $x \in R$	.41	.38
$1/2\sqrt{3}$ for $|x| \leq \sqrt{3}$ 0 $\quad$ for $|x| > \sqrt{3}$	.49	.49
$e^{-2|x|}/\sqrt{2}$ $x \in R$	.20	.20
$\frac{1}{\pi} \cdot \frac{1}{1+x^2}$ $x \in R$	.41	.40

76

ourselves here with merely giving the definition. The measure is called the Kullback-Liebler information statistic.

$$J(f,\hat{f}) = \int\{f(x)\log f(x) - f(x)\log \hat{f}(x)\}dx.$$

While it is easy to go on defining, if not choosing between, criteria such as those described above it will not have escaped the reader's notice that it will often be difficult to apply them in practice because f is unknown (and if it were known there would be no need to go through this whole process). In the next section we face this problem and present a general method which can be applied with any criterion based on comparing $\hat{f}$ with f. We have set the description of this method apart, first because of its great generality in principle, and second because it seems at present to be much more widely applied than the methods of Silverman or Breiman et al.

For completeness we should also at least mention a method which has been proposed by several authors (e.g. Tapia and Thompson, 1978) for finding smoothing parameters for the univariate case. (This means that it is of limited applicability for us, although we could conceivably apply the method to the marginals). The method is, quite simply, to plot graphs of the estimated pdf for different h values. The final h is selected by choosing a graph which looks neither too irregular nor too smooth.

3.4   CROSS VALIDATION

To provide some motivation for the general method we will introduce in this section let us first consider the straightforward maximum likelihood approach. The maximum likelihood estimate of h is that value which maximises

$$J_{ML} = \prod_{i=1}^{n} \hat{f}(x_i) \qquad (3.4.1)$$

However, consider the case of K monotonic decreasing with increasing $|x|$ and $K(x) >= 0$ for all x. Then

$$J_{ML} = \prod_{i=1}^{n} \{\sum_{j=1}^{n} \frac{1}{nh} K(\frac{x_i - x_j}{h})\}$$

$$>= \prod_{i=1}^{n} \{\frac{1}{nh} K(\frac{x_i - x_i}{h})\}$$

by the non-negativity of K. Thus

$$J_{ML} >= \prod_{i=1}^{n} \frac{1}{nh} \max_{x} K(x)$$

by the monotonicity of K. Consequently (ignoring the trivial $K(x) \equiv 0$), as $h \downarrow 0$ so $J_{ML} \to \infty$. The maximising value of h will be h = 0. This is far from an ideal choice for our purposes, leading to an estimate $\hat{f}$ consisting of a series of probability spikes located at the $x_i (1 = 1,...,n)$ and being zero elsewhere.

The difficulty obviously arises because of the appearance of $K((x_i - x_i)/h)$ in the above. Noting this, several authors (for example, Habbema, Hermans, and Van den Broek, 1974; Duin, 1976) have suggested modifying the straightforward likelihood function J above by replacing $\hat{f}$ by

$$f^*_{(i)}(x_i) = \frac{1}{n-1} \sum_{\substack{j=1 \\ j \neq i}}^{n} \frac{1}{h} K(\frac{x_i - x_j}{h})$$

Now $(x_i - x_i)$ cannot occur (unless $x_i = x_j$ for some $i \neq j$, an event possessing zero probability for continuous variables).

This approach leads to effective h estimates and also has an appealing and elegant simplicity. But in what way is it a general approach, and how can it be applied to other criteria discussed in the preceding section? To answer these questions, it is easiest to work backwards. So, we begin with the Kullback-Liebler criterion introduced at the end of Section 3.3. We then have

$$J(f,\hat{f}) = \int f(x)\log f(x)/\hat{f}(x)dx \qquad (3.4.2)$$

Now, since $f(x)$ is unknown let us replace it by the observed distribution $\phi(x)$ where

$$\phi(x) = \sum_{j=1}^{n} \delta_j(x)$$

where $\delta_j(x)$ is the Dirac delta function located at x_j. Thus

$$J_1 = \int \sum_j \delta_j(x) \, \log \sum_i \delta_i(x)/\hat{f}(x)dx$$

$$= \sum_j \log \sum_i \delta_i(x_j)/\hat{f}(x_j) \qquad (3.4.3)$$

$$= \sum_j \log \sum_i \delta_i(x_j) - \sum_j \log \hat{f}(x_j)$$

The first term is constant (though of indeterminate value) and will not change as h is changed. Consequently, we can minimise J_1 by minimising

$$J_2 = -\sum_j \log \hat{f}(x_j).$$

This is equivalent to maximising

$$J_3 = \prod_j \hat{f}(x_j).$$

which is the standard maximum likelihood solution of (3.4.1). In other words, minimising the Kullback-Liebler distance between the observed distribution and the kernel estimate by choice of h is equivalent to finding h by maximising the likelihood function. This, as we have already noted, is of limited practical use since it leads to an estimated h of zero. In view of this, we modify the Kullback-Liebler distance (3.4.2) to become

$$J^* = \int f(x) \log f(x)/f^*(x)dx$$

where $f^*(x) = f^*_{(i)}(x_i)$ for $i = 1,...,n$ and is undefined elsewhere. Then, following the same argument as before, we replace $f(x)$ by the observed distribution $\phi(x)$ and can show that minimising

$$J^*_1 = \int \phi(x) \log \phi(x)/f^*(x)dx \qquad (3.4.4)$$

leads to the same h as maximising

$$J^*_3 = \prod_j f^*_{(j)}(x_j) \qquad (3.4.5)$$

In summary, if we modify the Kullback-Liebler criterion introduced in Section 3.3, so that instead of measuring the distance between f and $\hat{f}$ we measure the difference between ϕ and f^*, we obtain reasonable results.

Now the Kullback-Liebler measure is just one of many introduced earlier and this suggests that the same approach might be applied for any of these measures. That is, we replace a general measure $J(f,\hat{f})$ between f and $\hat{f}$ by the form $J(\phi,f^*)$. In fact a clearer idea of this can be obtained from (3.4.4) as follows. We have to choose that h which minimises

$$\int \{\sum_j \delta_j(x) \log \sum_k \delta_k(x)/f^*(x)\}dx$$

and the same h minimises

$$\frac{1}{n} \sum_i \{\sum_j \delta_j(x_i) \log \sum_k \delta_k(x_i)/f^*(x_i)\}.$$

We can express this in the general form

$$\frac{1}{n} \sum_i L\{\phi(x_i),f^*(x_i)\}$$

where

$$L\{\phi(x_i), f^*(x_i)\} = \Sigma_j \delta_j(x_i) \log \frac{\Sigma_k \delta_k(x_i)}{f^*(x_i)}$$

L is the Kullback-Liebler distance between the observed function ϕ and the modified estimate f^* at the single point x_i. The overall J criterion is thus an average of these distances. And this is how we can generalise the approach. The steps for an arbitrary loss function $L(a,b)$ are as follows:

(i)   For each x_i, $i = 1, \ldots, n$ calculate

$$L_i = L\{\phi(x_i), f^*(x_i)\}$$

(ii) Average the L_i to give

$$J = \frac{1}{n} \sum_{i=1}^{n} L_i$$

(iii) Iterate through (i) and (ii) to find the h which minimises J.

As another example, take the criterion function

$$\int \{f(x) - \hat{f}(x)\}^2 dx.$$

Step (i) gives

$$L_i = \{\delta_i(x_i) - f^*_{(i)}(x_i)\}^2$$

which for our purposes is equivalent to

$$L_i = f^*_{(i)}(x_i)^2.$$

Step (ii) then gives

$$J = \frac{1}{n} \sum_{i=1}^{n} f^*_{(i)}(x_i)^2.$$

The method of parameter estimation described above - termed cross validation - is of much more general applicability than our development might suggest. Stone (1974) describes the more general context (and see the next Chapter for further discussion).

So far the emphasis has been on selecting h and K by optimising some measure of fit of the estimates of the individual class conditional distributions to the true distributions (or practically feasible approaches to this). In the preceding section we did, however, make a passing reference to the use of the estimated misclassification rate for this purpose. Estimation of misclassification rate has been the subject of intensive research over the years and, although a difficult problem, seems to have been adequately solved. Methods are discussed in Chapter 6. One of the methods, popularly termed the leaving-one-out method, is in fact an application of cross-validation to error rate estimation.

Although choosing h by minimising the misclassification rate may seem to be the best approach, in some circumstances there are convincing arguments against it. We leave these to the next section.

The astute reader will have noticed that although our concern will usually be with the multidimensional case, most of the preceding discussion has been in terms of $d = 1$. There are several reasons for this. One is the almost universal use of product kernels. Here a separate h can be estimated for each dimension - so the $d = 1$ results apply. Moreover, since most of the advanced theoretical work concentrates on the univariate case it would be an incorrect reflection of the state of the discipline were we not to do likewise. Given that each variable is to be studied separately, any of the preceding methods may be applied. Note, however, that in the case of continuous variables (unlike that of binary variables) a prior normalisation of each marginal sample standard deviation will permit one to use the same h in each dimension (but see Section 2.3). One can, of course, combine the individual marginal optimisation criteria into a single criterion (for example, by multiplying them together).

Apart from this completely general usage of any estimation method via the marginals, we can also attempt a more fundamental generalisation to d > 1. Thus it will not be difficult to replace x by $\underline{x}$ and x_i by $\underline{x}_i$ in much of the preceding discussion. For example in the modified maximum likelihood method (Kullback-Liebler cross-validation) we choose h to maximise

$$\prod_{i=1}^{n} f^*_{(i)}(\underline{x}_i) = \prod_{i=1}^{n} \frac{1}{n-1} \sum_{\substack{j=1 \\ j \neq i}}^{n} K(\underline{x}_i, \underline{x}_j).$$

The fact that there are two approaches to generalisation naturally raises the question of which is the better. We have already discussed this a little in Section 3.2 (Sacks and Ylvisaker, 1981) and will discuss it further in the next section.

3.5   TO CHOOSE A METHOD

In the preceding section we demonstrated how superficially impracticable estimation methods could be converted into usable algorithms, and at the end of this chapter we note which methods are most commonly applied in practice. However, we must remember that kernel discriminant analysis and kernel pattern recognition are relatively new areas. Thus commonly applied methods need not be the best methods. More work is needed to determine in what circumstances the different methods of estimating the smoothing parameters should be applied. Beyond this, however, it seems fair to say that more work is needed to determine just how critical the choice of h is (and, indeed, in what circumstances it is critical). In this section, we discuss these problems and summarise the work that has been done.

First note that conceptual difficulties are encountered when we try to compare the performance of estimators. There is, of course, the obvious difficulty with real data that we have no knowledge of the true density - so we cannot tell in absolute terms how good an estimator is (so, in turn, we cannot tell how effective the estimation method is). Less obvious, but perhaps more serious, is a problem which applies to both real and synthetic data - even though in the latter case the true density is known. This is simply the perennial problem of how to compare estimators (equivalently, estimation methods). The point is, as we discussed at the beginning of Section 3.3, that estimation methods work by minimising some difference measure between the estimate $\hat{f}$ and the true function (or some approximation to it). Thus in a comparison using some criterion J as the assessment criterion, we might expect the method which used J as the difference measure to emerge as the apparent best. (Note that this may not be a foregone conclusion since for estimation we minimise $J(\hat{f}, f^*)$ where f^* is an approximation to f (for example, the sample distribution) and for assessment on synthetic data we minimise $J(\hat{f}, f)$). However, notwithstanding the previous parenthesis, we are presented with something of a dilemma. If we introduce another criterion, J_c, to compare estimators, one is naturally led to the suggestion that J_c should be used in the estimation in the first place. (If the assessment is based on J_c because J_c measures that aspect of the difference in which we are most interested, then naturally we should choose h by optimising J_c). The consequence of this would seem to be that we should use, as the estimation criterion, that criterion which we ultimately wish to use.

At this juncture it is useful to note that the comparison of estimators can, for our purposes, be made on two distinct bases. One can either consider individual class conditional distributions and assess how well each of the methods reproduces the individual probabilities, or one can proceed right to the final aim and see how the estimators perform in discrimination. Virtually all of the discussion so far in this Chapter has assumed the former approach. Apart from reflecting the emphasis in the literature, is there any reason for this? That the answer is yes will become apparent below. However, to return to the above discussion, the introduction of the discrimination performance does not resolve our dilemma. It is subject to exactly the same arguments as the goodness of fit J criteria. If, for example misclassification rate is to be used as an assessment criterion then why not choose the h which minimises the misclassification rate? The suggestion that this approach cannot be applied to real data no longer holds water in view of the recently developed error rate estimation methods outlined in Chapter 6.

But perhaps it seems that this does solve the dilemma. And, indeed, if misclassification rate minimisation is our ultimate objective then the problem has been solved. However, more often than not misclassification rate is merely a default criterion and usually we will be interested in a more complex loss of function. Again, if we can specify this function our problem is solved. But all too often researchers will be loath to specify a loss function ab initio. At least, that is the experience of the present author after many fruitless attempts to persuade researchers from a variety of disciplines to provide cost - and hence loss - functions.

In choosing between the two types of assessment (and estimation) criteria - goodness of fit versus discrimination performance - there are other considerations which should be taken into account. Accurate probability estimates, as opposed to accurate classification loss rates, can have important advantages for more sophisticatd discrimination and pattern recognition problems. For example, if incomplete vectors are common then the capability of making reasonable marginal subspace classifications is important - and operations equivalent to multivariate integration are performed (see Chapter 6), with resultant multiplied inaccuracy if the overall pdfs are poorly estimated. Similar remarks apply to the implementation of the reject option - which depends on density estimation and which is discussed in Chapter 6. Finally, concentrating on individual classes allows us to implement multivariate loss functions (for example, functions which examine both types of misclassification simultaneously in a two class problem) as well as leaving us with the flexibility to try different loss functions at a later stage.

In summary, it seems that although an ideal answer to how we should assess the relative performance of the estimators is not available, the following points can be made:

(i)   If a loss function can be specified a priori then use this.

(ii)   Otherwise use a goodness of fit measure - and we believe that forms like (3.3.6) are most suited in general, though any available problem specific knowledge should obviously be utilised.

An example of how the optimum choice of λ (the smoothing parameter for a particular class of categorical variable kernels) is affected by different choices of loss function for a real data set is given in Table 4.3 and is discussed in Chapter 4. With different loss functions different λ's are best, and moreover the range of λ over which the classifier performs well is strongly dependent on the loss function. We now present a preliminary investigation into this question, that is the question of how sensitive the results are to the choice of smoothing parameter for the special case of the 0/1 loss function.

We consider the special case of two classes and see how the misclassification rate changes with h for various d, π_i, $f_i(\underline{x})$, and separations between the classes. Since in the simulations reported below $f_1(\underline{x}) = f_2(\underline{x})$ except for a shift in location there is no disadvantage (in fact there is an advantage) in taking the same smoothing parameter for each class, as we have done. Before studying the simulation results it is useful to look at some special cases which can be easily recognised on theoretical grounds:

1. L. First consider the case of $h \to \infty$. Then the estimate $\hat{f}(\underline{x})$ tends more and more to resemble a single K function. Take the normal kernel as an example. We have

$$\hat{f}(x) = \frac{1}{nh\sqrt{2\pi}} \sum_{i=1}^{n} \exp\{-(x-x_i)^2/2h^2\}$$

As h increases so $(x-x_i)^2/2h^2 \to 0$ for all x_i. Thus if δ^2 is some kind of average of the $(x-x_i)^2$ we can replace $(x-x_i)^2$ by δ^2 for all i with an error which can be made arbitrarily small by taking h large enough. Hence

$$\hat{f}(x) \simeq \frac{1}{nh\sqrt{2\pi}} \sum_{i=1}^{n} \exp\{-\delta^2/2h^2\}$$

where the accuracy of the approximation depends on h and the size of the $(x-x_i)^2$. So finally

$$f(x) \simeq \frac{1}{h\sqrt{2\pi}} \exp \{-\delta^2/2h^2\}.$$

Thus, for normal classes with equal h in each class, as h increases so the decision surface becomes more and more similar to a linear hyperplane. It is interesting to see what happens to this hyperplane as h continues to increase. Again we simplify to the d = 1 case.

Suppose that h is large enough for us adequately to approximate each class estimate by a single normal distribution. Then the decision point lies at the solution of

$$\frac{\pi_1}{h\sqrt{2\pi}} \exp \{-(x-\mu_1)^2/2h^2\} = \frac{\pi_2}{h\sqrt{2\pi}} \exp \{-(x-\mu_2)^2/2h^2\}.$$

Without loss of generality we shall suppose $\pi_1 < \pi_2$ and $\mu_1 < \mu_2$. Now we must solve

$$\frac{\pi_1}{\pi_2} \exp \{(\mu_2-\mu_1)(\mu_2+\mu_1-2x)/2h^2\} = 1$$

giving

$$x = \tfrac{1}{2}\{(\mu_2+\mu_1) - (2h^2\ln \pi_2/\pi_1)/(\mu_2-\mu_1)\}$$

And as h increases so x moves smoothly along the line beyond the class with smaller prior. Eventually (h = ∞) the whole line (or, more generally, the whole space R^d) will be allocated to the class with the larger prior. That is, in general, in the limit as h → ∞ we have

$$L = \min \{\pi_1, \pi_2\}.$$

Note the special case with $\pi_1 = \pi_2$. Then $x = (\mu_1+\mu_2)/2$ is independent of h.

2.   B.   The Bayes optimum error rate is attained if we classify a point $\underline{x}$ as

$$\underline{x} \ \varepsilon \ \text{class 1 if} \quad \pi_1 f_1(\underline{x}) > \pi_2 f_2(\underline{x})$$

$$\underline{x} \ \varepsilon \ \text{class 2 if} \quad \pi_2 f_2(\underline{x}) > \pi_1 f_1(\underline{x})$$

The error rate is then

$$B = \int \min_i \{\pi_i f_i(\underline{x})\}\{\pi_1 f_1(\underline{x}) + \pi_2 f_2(\underline{x})\}dx$$

This is also the limiting case as $n \to \infty$ and $h = h(n) \to 0$.

3.   S.   For common kernels such as the normal, for a fixed sample size, as h shrinks so the   estimate becomes dominated by the nearest neighbour to $\underline{x}$.   (This is easily seen for the   normal case by noting that if u > w then

$$\frac{\exp(-u^2/2h^2)/h}{\exp(-w^2/2h^2)/h} \to 0$$

as $h \to 0$).   Thus if the nearest neighbour to $\underline{x}$ is not far from $\underline{x}$ we can approximate the probability that $\underline{x}$ will be classified into class i by

$$\pi_i f_i(\underline{x})/\{\pi_1 f_1(\underline{x}) + \pi_2 f_2(\underline{x})\}.$$

Now, the probability of observing a point at $\underline{x}$ which belongs to class i is $\pi_i f_i(\underline{x})$.   The overall error rate is thus

$$S = \int \pi_1 f_1(\underline{x}) \frac{\pi_2 f_2(\underline{x})}{\pi_1 f_1(\underline{x}) + \pi_2 f_2(\underline{x})} dx + \int \pi_2 f_2(\underline{x}) \frac{\pi_1 f_1(\underline{x})}{\pi_1 f_1(\underline{x}) + \pi_2 f_2(\underline{x})} \ dx$$

$$= 2\int \pi_1 f_1(\underline{x})\pi_2 f_2(\underline{x})/\{\pi_1 f_1(\underline{x}) + \pi_2 f_2(\underline{x})\}d\underline{x}$$

Figure 3.3 shows plots of L, B, and S for two standard multivariate normal distributions in d dimensions, the first located at the origin and the second at $(\mu, 0, \ldots, 0)$ $(\mu = 0.2, 1.0, 2.0)$, for different values of π_1.   Note that if $f_1(\underline{x}) = f_2(\underline{x})$ then B = L and if $\pi_1 = \pi_2$ while

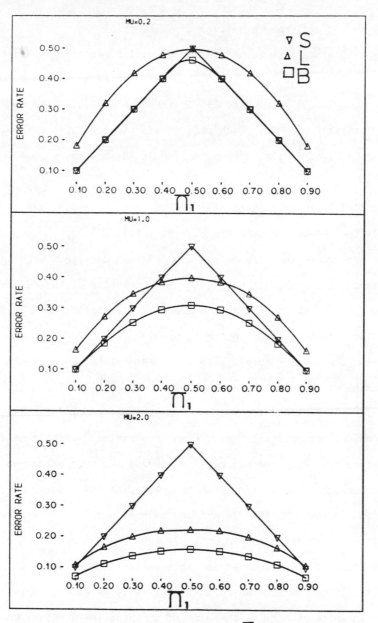

Figure 3.3 Error rate against π_1 for two multivariate normal distributions with $\underline{\Sigma}_1 = \underline{\Sigma}_2 = \underline{I}$ separated by distance μ=0.2,1.0,2.0. The vertical axis ranges from 0.10 to 0.50 and the horizontal axis from 0.1 to 0.9.

$f_1(\underline{x}) = f_2(\underline{x} + \underline{v})$ then $L = \frac{1}{2}$.

Figure 3.4 shows plots of misclassification rate for two multivariate normal classes with identity covariance matrices and means $\underline{0}$ for class 1 and $(\mu, 0, \ldots, 0)$ for class 2. μ takes values 0.2, 1.0 and 2.0. d takes values 2, 5, 10. Each page shows three values of sample size: top, $n_1 = 2$, $n_2 = 8$; middle, $n_1 = 5$, $n_2 = 20$; bottom, $n_1 = 10$, $n_2 = 40$. Thus $\pi_1 = 0.2$.

Figure 3.5 is as Figure 3.4 except that $\pi_1 = 0.5$ (and the design sample for the middle plot has $n_1 = n_2 = 10$).

For each curve in Figures 3.4 and 3.5 ten data sets were generated for each n, d, μ combination (a data set consisting of the design set and a 100 point test set) and the average misclassification rates were calculated to be plotted in the figures.

First consider Figure 3.4(a). These plots show the error rate beginning at about the S level (0.32 for $\mu = 0.2$, 0.27 for $\mu = 1.0$, and 0.16 for $\mu = 2.0$) and finishing at the L level (0.2). The behaviour in between depends on sample size n and separation μ. In general, as h increases from 0, the error rate drops and may drop below the L level (of course, if μ is great enough the rate will start below L).

As we increase d this behaviour becomes modified. A larger n is required to produce a correspondingly low error rate.

The shape of these curves is interesting and is being investigated but it will not be studied further here as it is not our chief concern. The main interest here is the size of the range of h values which give an acceptably low error rate. For d = 2 with small sample sizes and large separation (Figure 3.4(a), (b), (c) lowest plots on all three graphs) a fairly large range of h is acceptable - provided h is not too large. As n increases, however, (for example, the bottom curve on Figure 3.4(c)) this range becomes shorter. This is perhaps to be expected since the optimum h decreases with increasing n. For classes which are less well separated, of course, no h gives much improvement over choosing the class with the largest prior. It is interesting to note, however, that small h (nearest neighbour type performance) can give much worse performance and is to be avoided in this case.

As d increases larger sample sizes are needed to produce a correspondingly low error rate. Note that in all cases the lowest rate achieved should be compared with the lowest achievable - the Bayes rates. These are 0.20 (μ = 0.2), 0.19 (μ = 1.0) and 0.11 (μ = 2.0).

The plots for equal priors (Figure 3.5) show a completely different set of shapes. As far as sensitivity goes we can summarise the relevant aspects by saying that h should be large. This is not surprising in view of our comment (in the discussion of L above) that when $\pi_1 = \pi_2$ and $f_i(\underline{x})$ are multivariate normal differing only in the mean and with identity covariance matrices then the kernel decision surface tends to the optimum separating hyperplane as $h \to \infty$.

Figures 3.6 and 3.7 show similar plots for two lognormal distributions, differing only in the mean. For π_1 = 0.2 (Figure 3.6) and d = 2, if the classes are well separated (lowest plots on each graph) then any h in the range 0-0.4 seems reasonable. For less well separated classes it seems that any h which is large enough - that is, classifying all points to the class with the greatest prior - is the best we can do. Thus the choice of h seems to depend on the separation between the classes. This sort of pattern follows through to the π_1 = 0.2, d = 5 and 10 cases, except that it becomes harder to do better than L.   Indeed, for d = 10 none of the   curves drop below   an error rate of 0.2.

The lognormal π_1 = 0.5 case (Figure 3.7) shows that a fairly short range of small h yields good results. (Note the horizontal axis has been rescaled on Figure 3.7).   The difference between the π_1 = 0.5 cases for normal and lognormal classes (Figures 3.5 and 3.7) are presumably due at least in part to the fact that normal product kernels were used.   The implications of this for the choice of kernel shape for the classification are currently being investigated.

Other authors have commented in passing about the sensitivity to choice of h.   Remme, Habbema and Hermans (1980) present graphs of h versus a performance measure for

(a)   two normal classes with equal covariance matrices,

(b)   two normal classes with different covariance matrices,

(c)   two lognormal distributions,

(d)   two normal mixture distributions.

Their performance measure was the percentage of test elements which had estimates $\hat{f}(\underline{x})$ in the correct one of the three intervals {0,0.1}, {0.1,0.9}, {0.9,1.0}.   That is, the percentage of test elements for which both $f_i(\underline{x})$ and $\hat{f}_i(\underline{x})$ fell in the same one of these three intervals. Their graphs show that h is more critical in the lognormal and mixture case. It is worth noting here that their main purpose in presenting these graphs was to study the performance of the modified maximum likelihood method of estimating h. As we might expect in view of earlier discussions, the method does not perform very well with the lognormal distribution.

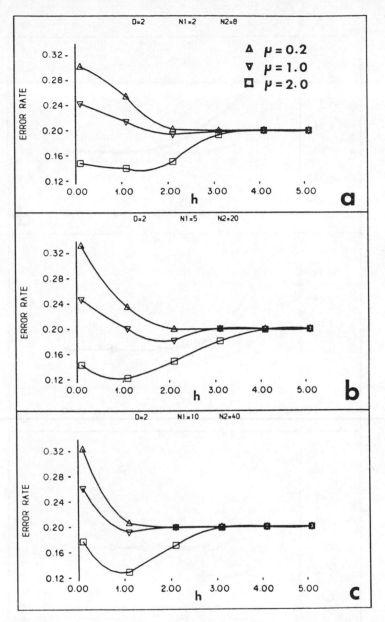

Figure 3.4 Error rates (vertical axis, range
0.12-0.32) against h (horizontal axis, range
0-5) for normal product kernel classifier on
two multivariate normal classes.
(a) d=2, π_1 =0.2, n_1 =2.
(b) d=2, π_1 =0.2, n_1 =5.
(c) d=2, π_1 =0.2, n_1 =10.

94

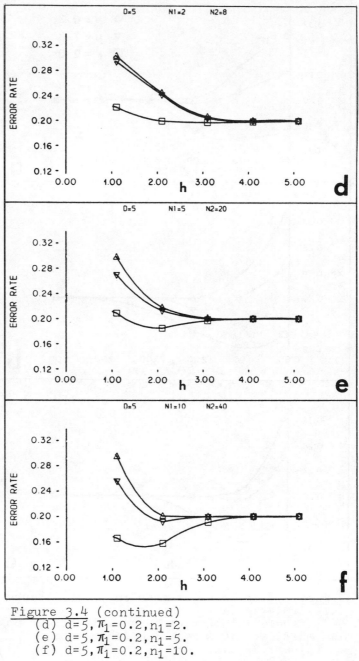

Figure 3.4 (continued)
(d) d=5, π_1=0.2, n_1=2.
(e) d=5, π_1=0.2, n_1=5.
(f) d=5, π_1=0.2, n_1=10.

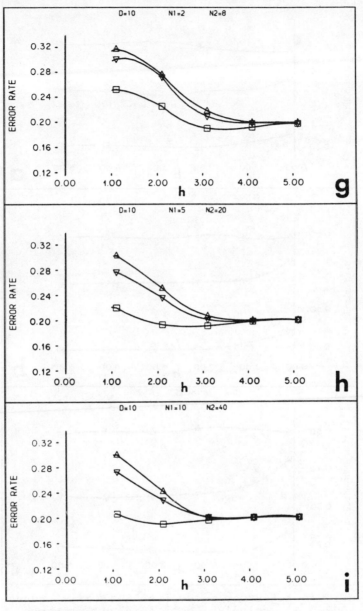

Figure 3.4 (continued)
(g) d=10, $\pi_1=0.2$, $n_1=2$.
(h) d-10, $\pi_1=0.2$, $n_1=5$.
(i) d=10, $\pi_1=0.2$, $n_1=10$.

96

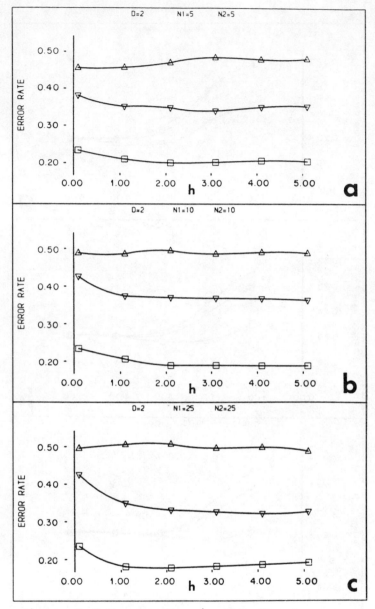

Figure 3.5 Error rates (vertical axis, range
0.2-0.5) against h (horizontal axis, range
0-5) for normal product kernel classifier on
two multivariate normal classes. For symbols
see Figure 3.4.
   (a) d=2, π_1=0.5, n_1=5.
   (b) d=2, π_1=0.5, n_1=10.
   (c) d=2, π_1=0.5, n_1=25.

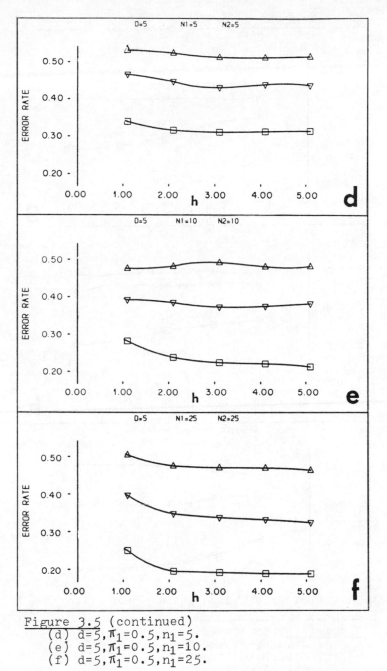

Figure 3.5 (continued)
(d) d=5,π_1=0.5,n_1=5.
(e) d=5,π_1=0.5,n_1=10.
(f) d=5,π_1=0.5,n_1=25.

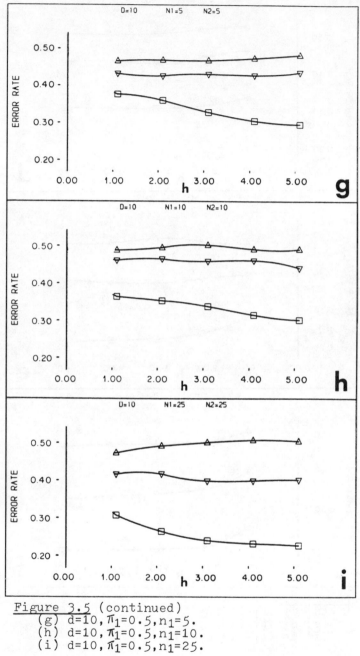

Figure 3.5 (continued)
(g) d=10, π_1=0.5, n_1=5.
(h) d=10, π_1=0.5, n_1=10.
(i) d=10, π_1=0.5, n_1=25.

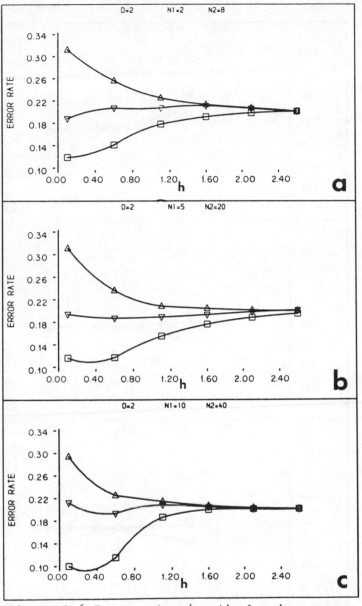

Figure 3.6 Error rates (vertical axis, range
0.10-0.34) against h (horizontal axis, range
0-2.6) for normal product kernel classifier on
two multivariate lognormal distributions.
(a) d=2,π_1=0.2,n_1=2.
(b) d=2,π_1=0.2,n_1=5.
(c) d=2,π_1=0.2,n_1=10.

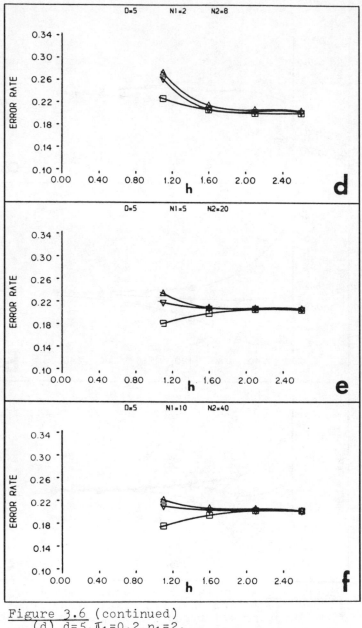

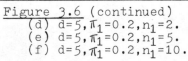

Figure 3.6 (continued)
    (d) $d=5, \pi_1=0.2, n_1=2$.
    (e) $d=5, \pi_1=0.2, n_1=5$.
    (f) $d=5, \pi_1=0.2, n_1=10$.

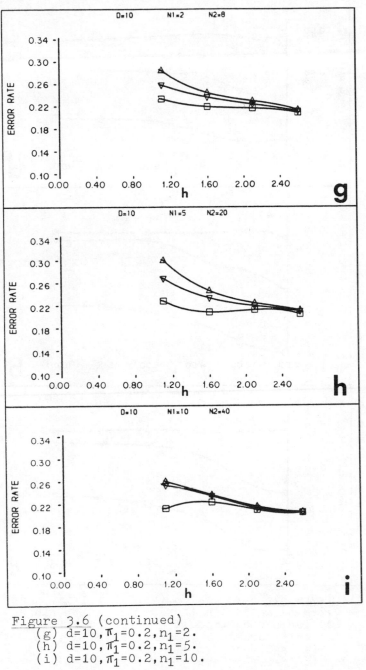

Figure 3.6 (continued)
  (g) d=10, π_1=0.2, n_1=2.
  (h) d=10, π_1=0.2, n_1=5.
  (i) d=10, π_1=0.2, n_1=10.

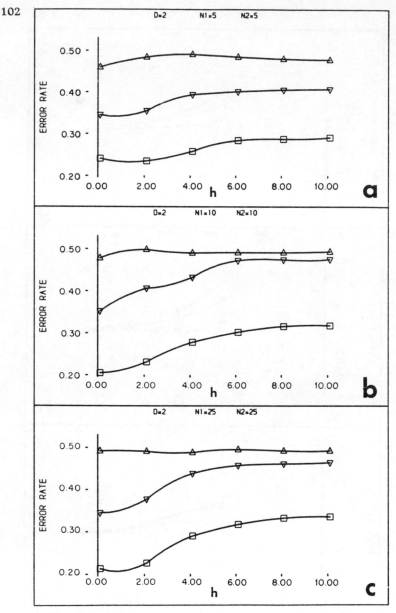

Figure 3.7 Error rates (vertical axis, range 0.2-0.5) against h (horizontal axis, range 0-10) for normal product kernel classifier on two multivariate lognormal distributions.
(a) $d=2, \pi_1=0.5, n_1=5$.
(b) $d=2, \pi_1=0.5, n_1=10$.
(c) $d=2, \pi_1=0.5, n_1=25$.

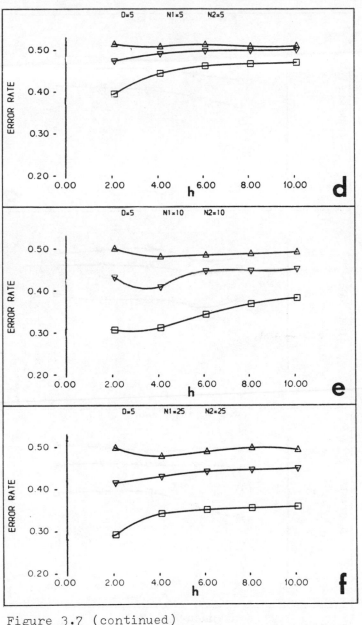

Figure 3.7 (continued)
(d) $d=5, \pi_1=0.5, n_1=5$.
(e) $d=5, \pi_1=0.5, n_1=10$.
(f) $d=5, \pi_1=0.5, n_1=25$.

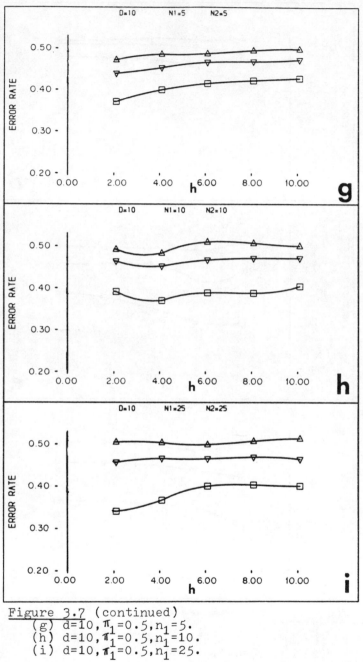

Figure 3.7 (continued)
   (g) d=10, π_1=0.5, n_1=5.
   (h) d=10, π_1=0.5, n_1=10.
   (i) d=10, π_1=0.5, n_1=25.

Van Ness and Simpson (1976), during the course of some extensive simulations comparing classical linear and quadratic discriminant analysis as well as kernel methods, also made some comments about sensitivity of results to choice of h. Their data come from two normal classes with identical covariance matrices and equal priors. They noted that the optimal h (optimal in the sense of minimising misclassification rate) increased with dimensionality and between class separability, although the sensitivity to the latter was very slight at higher dimensions. A typical plot of their results shows misclassification rate falling sharply as h increases when h is small and then increasing very slowly as h grows large. They also used the same h for both classes. (Compare Figure 3.5). This is, as we have already commented, not surprising in view of the behaviour of the decision surface with normal kernels as h increases.

A similar plot is shown in Specht (1967, his figure 2). This is derived from real data rather than simulated data with a known distribution

It is interesting to comment here on the results of Fryer (1976). He studied MSE, MISE and EMSE, the latter defined by

$$\int MSE(f,\hat{f})f(x)dx$$

for univariate kernel estimates using normal kernels to estimate a normal density. Using analytic methods, he produced plots of contours of MSE on axes of $y(= (x-\mu)/\sigma)$ and $g(= h/\sigma)$ where the normal density being estimated has mean μ and standard deviation σ. There are a number of points about these graphs which are relevant to our discussion of sensitivity. First, for small n the MSE is insensitive to g, provided g is larger than the MSE optimal choice. Thus a plot of

MSE against g would, for small n, produce curves similar in shape to those of error rate described above from Van Ness and Simpson (1976) and Specht (1967). Secondly, as y increases so the sensitivity of MSE to g decreases. This is not surprising when one recalls that as y increases we are moving out to the sparse tails of the normal $f(\underline{x})$. The way in which a larger g (and so h) should be chosen as the distribution becomes sparser is clearly demonstrated in these plots.

For the simple kernel method we require a single fixed h for a given n. Fryer presents a table of the h's which minimise max MSE, MISE and EMSE for various sample sizes (and using normal kernels to estimate univariate normal densities). This is reproduced (with permission) as Table 3.8. As Fryer remarks, the EMSE and MISE based g 's are larger than the max MSE based g so that the result should not be too far from optimal by virtue of the first property of the graphs discussed above.

Fryer has extended this study to the case when f(x) is a two component normal mixture, and we discuss this below.

In Van Ness (1979) the author takes the first step in generalising the results of Van Ness and Simpson (1976) by considering the same situation as Van Ness and Simpson (1976) except that the covariance matrices are now $\underline{I}$ and $\underline{I}/2$ instead of both being $\underline{I}$. In this case the optimal decision surface is no longer linear so we would expect a greater sensitivity to h when h was not small. This was indeed observed: as h increased so the error rate deteriorated more sharply than was the case in their earlier paper. (Again the same h was used in each class.) Van Ness (1979) also studied the use of different h's for each class. Rather than estimating each h separately, however, he estimated h for class 1 and then set h for class 2 proportional to

TABLE 3.8

Optimal values of $g = h/\sigma$ for estimating a univariate normal density $f(x) = N(\mu,\sigma^2)$ using normal kernels $K(x) = N(0,h^2)$.

Criterion	1	5	10	50	100	500	1000
				Sample Size, n			
Min (Max MSE)	1.0596	0.7439	0.6388	0.4502	0.3881	0.2764	0.2393
Min (EMSE)	1.2980	0.8794	0.7476	0.5174	0.4431	0.3168	0.2707
Min (MISE)	1.4142	0.9029	0.7585	0.5199	0.4455	0.3150	0.2723

this, where the constant of proportionality is given by an estimate of the ratio of the standard deviations of the two classes. Plots of proportion of the test set correctly classified are more sharply peaked when h is different for the two classes. Moreover the modes in this case are higher than the modes for the case when the same h is used. (Van Ness used a cross validatory type of estimation method for h and found it led to h estimates much closer to the mode in the different h case than in the same h case.) It is also of interest to note that, when the same h is used, as it increases so it is the class 1 points (i.e. those from the less peaked distribution) which tend to be misclassified.

These comparisons are taken a stage further in Van Ness (1980), where the two normal classes are permitted to have different (not proportional) diagonal matrices (see also Chapter 7). Van Ness considered a number of different kernels for use in this case and settled for normal kernels with covariance matrices proportional to the diagonal matrix of estimated variances for each class (c.f. Remme et al, 1980). The constant of proportionality was chosen by a cross validatory method. Van Ness (1980) presents a plot showing how the error rate varies with different values of this constant. (In fact he plots the percentage correctly classified.) The error rate curve is U-shaped - and increase after the lowest point is quite marked and not gradual as in Van Ness and Simpson (1976). This is perhaps to be expected. Another interesting feature of the plot is that it becomes sharper as d decreases. Van Ness also notes that the estimated best value of this constant of proportionality decreases as d increases. He suggests that this might be due to the fact that less smoothing is needed as more discriminating information is added.

Fryer (1976) has studied the sensitivity of MISE to choice of h when f(x) is a two component univariate normal mixture and normal kernels are used. Sample plots are presented in Fryer (1976), from which it is clear that the optimal g (= h/σ_1, σ_1 being the standard deviation of the first of the normal mixture components) are not very different from those obtained when f(x) is assumed to be normal with standard deviation σ_1.

Scott and Factor (1981) made some simulation comparisons of the modified maximum likelihood method of estimating h (i.e. the Kullback-Liebler cross validatory method) with the iterative asymptotic MISE minimisation method of Scott, Tapia and Thompson (1977) (Section 3.2). They consider d = 1 and 25 points from a normal distribution and d = 1 with a two component normal mixture. In general the modified maximum likelihood method out-performed the alternative method (as measured by MISE) although there was not a great difference in the results. One interesting point was that the Scott et al method produced degenerate solutions ($\hat{h}$ = 0) in 4 of the 200 simulations while the modified maximum likelihood method produced none. This is interesting because the method of Hall (1981) for binary data - a method which is conceptually very similar to that of Scott et al - was developed to avoid the problem of degenerate solutions which can arise with the modified maximum likelihood method if the binary data take certain forms (see Section 4.3.3).

Scott and Factor (1981) also studied the comparative sensitivity of the modified maximum likelihood method and the asymptotic MISE minimisation method. Note here a difference in terminology. In the above we have used the term sensitivity to indicate whether a performance measure did or did not depend critically on the choice of h. Scott and Factor, on the other hand "defined an insensitive data-based algorithm as one that produced values of the smoothing parameter that were nearly independent of the value of x" where x was an extra point added to the set of 25 generated according to the normal distribution. Using this definition of sensitivity the asymptotic MISE minimisation method was insensitive while the modified maximum likelihood method was very sensitive (as a startling graph in Scott and Factor, 1981, eloquently demonstrates). Note, of course, that sensitivity in this sense should be interpreted in the light of our earlier usage: though clearly one would be suspicious of a method which yielded wildly different h estimates for minor data modifications, it would not matter much provided these "wildly different h estimates" led to similar performance results.

This paper also provides a real data example indicating the point that if the data are grouped (or, more generally, if some $x_i = x_j$, $i \neq j$) then the modified maximum likelihood method will have a global maximum at h = 0. Provided the data are not too coarsely grouped other local maxima away from h = 0 will exist.

In Section 3.4 we noted that methods for estimating spread parameters in the multivariate case could be derived via two different kinds of generalisations of univariate approaches. We have performed some preliminary experiments to compare these two generalisations. First, let us recapitulate the methods - and for simplicity we shall assume that each class has a single h (not a different h for each variable).

(i) A fundamental generalisation. To illustrate consider the modified maximum likelihood method. Here we estimate h by maximising

$$\sum_{\substack{i=1 \\ j \neq i}}^{n} \sum_{j=1}^{n} \prod_{k=1}^{d} K(x_{ik}, x_{jk}; h) \qquad (3.5.1)$$

(ii) Each variable is considered separately and they are combined by multiplying them together. Here the objective function is

$$\prod_{k=1}^{d} \prod_{i=1}^{n} \sum_{\substack{j=1 \\ j \neq i}}^{n} K(x_{ik}, x_{jk}; h) \qquad (3.5.2)$$

Note that in (3.5.1) and (3.5.2) we have simplified things by dropping $(n-1)^{-1}$ factors since these remain constant as h changes. Of course, any of the other objective functions discussed above could be applied in this way and it is possible that with other functions the results outlined below might not be true.

To investigate the performance of smoothing parameters derived by optimising these two criteria a number of simulations were carried out. The first set involved two multivariate normal classes with identity covariance matrices, one located at the origin and one a distance μ from the origin. We used three values of μ (0.2, 1.0, 2.0) and three numbers of variables (d = 2,5,10). For each μ, d combination 10 simulations were performed, with design set sizes $n_1 = n_2 = 10$ and test set sizes of 50 from each class. A normal product kernel was used and as expected the multivariate method usually gave a larger h (smoother estimate). In fact, in the 90 simulation runs carried out, the marginal method only led to a larger h 4 times. Table 3.9 shows the average misclassification rates over the 10 simulations in each of the 9 situations studied for the two kinds of estimates. In interpreting

112

TABLE 3.9

A comparison of two methods of estimating h in the multivariate case:
(a) from equation (3.5.1), (b) from equation (3.5.2). The figures
in the table give error rates. μ is the distance between the means of
the two normal classes. d is the number of variables.

(a)

		μ 0.2	1.0	2.0
	2	.511	.325	.127
d	5	.473	.240	.040
	10	.464	.179	.011

(b)

		μ 0.2	1.0	2.0
	2	.518	.341	.129
d	5	.471	.241	.041
	10	.464	.179	.011

the results one should bear in mind the comments made above and elsewhere about the performance of normal product kernel methods on data known to come from two multivariate normal classes. Most striking in the table is the similarity of the results. What difference there is favours method (i), this being better in 5 cases while method (ii) is better in only one (in the other 3 cases - when d = 10 - the methods gave identical results). This suggests that there is not much effective difference between the two methods - though more extensive simulations on different data sets must be run before such a conclusion can be anything but tentative.

The results of a similar set of comparisons for two lognormal distributions are given in Table 3.10 (still using normal product kernels). Here the multivariate method gives the lower average misclassification rate four times and the marginal method also gives the better result four times. They have an equal result for d = 10 and μ = 0.2. Again the conclusion seems to be that there is not much effective difference between the two methods.

To this author, at least, method (i) is the more appealing since it seems to be a more elegant generalisation to d > 1. Note that in both cases actual classifications will be based on the usual product kernel form (as used in (3.5.1)) and that it is not being suggested that an independence model of form (3.5.2) should be used as a classifier. The product over variables in (3.5.2) just serves to produce a single h - it is an averaging process. Other "averages" could be used in its place.

114

TABLE 3.10

As for Table 3.9, but using lognormal classes.

(a)

		0.2	μ 1.0	2.0
	2	.487	.374	.297
d	5	.457	.335	.219
	10	.468	.313	.075

(b)

		0.2	μ 1.0	2.0
	2	.493	.371	.294
d	5	.458	.331	.259
	10	.468	.293	.162

Apart from these comments, method (ii) does have advantages. In particular method (ii) will require less computational effort. Method (i) needs

$$M_1 = (d-1)(n-1)n + (n-1)$$

multiplications (where n is the number of design set elements in the class in question) and

$$M_2 = n(n-2)$$

additions. Method (ii) requires

$$M_3 = nd - 1$$

multiplications and

$$M_4 = (n-2)nd$$

additions. It is easy to see that if $d > 1$ then $M_1 > M_3$ and $M_2 < M_4$. Since multiplication is the slower operation this favours the use of the marginal method.

Many of the questions discussed in this section have at best tentative answers, and in some cases not even that. They are topics of current research by the present author and others. To conclude this section it seems appropriate to include a summary of the methods which are most frequently applied in practice at the moment. Their popularity implies nothing about their relative merit, of course.

(i) For continuous variables the most widely used kernel form is the normal kernel

$$K(x) = \frac{1}{h\sqrt{2\pi}} \exp \{-x^2/2h^2\}$$

(ii) For $d > 1$ (our main concern) product kernels are usually used.

(iii) Different smoothing parameters are used for each class.

(iv) Smoothing parameters proportional to the sample standard deviation for each class and variable are used.

(v) The constant of proportionality (different for each class by (iii)) are chosen by the modified maximum likelihood method.

3.6   LOCATION DEPENDENT SMOOTHING PARAMETERS

So far in this chapter we have discussed the choice of h based on the assumption that (for a given class and variable) the same h was used everywhere in the space of $\underline{x}$. This is not an ideal choice, as can be easily seen by comparing the estimate $\hat{f}(\underline{x})$ in regions of high and low probability density. Clearly the "optimum" h value determined by the methods of preceding sections will be some kind of compromise: in regions of high probability density h will be too large and will produce an oversmoothed estimate, while in regions of low density h will be too small, resulting in isolated peaks appearing in the estimate. To counter this effect a number of authors have investigated the use of h's which depend on the local density of sample points. Usually the local density is defined in terms of distance between a point and its kth nearest neighbour in the design set. Before we study these proposals in detail, however, let us see how this change affects the intuitive notions outlined in Section 2.1, and also see what the extra costs are in terms of computational requirements.

It is still true that, as described in Section 2.1, $\hat{f}(\underline{x})$ is an average of contributions, one from each sample point $\underline{x}_i$, i = 1,...,n. However, it is no longer true that the size of these contributions depends only on the distance between $\underline{x}$ and $\underline{x}_i$. Now the contribution from $\underline{x}_i$ depends also on the local density near $\underline{x}_i$. This means that the so-called "variable kernel" estimate lacks a certain symmetry possessed by the "fixed kernel" estimate. In the latter the contribution to the estimate at $\underline{x}_i$ from a point $\underline{x}_j$ is the same as the contribution to the estimate at $\underline{x}_j$ from a point $\underline{x}_i$. In the former, however, these two contributions will generally not be the same. As far as computation goes, no great additional burden has been introduced at the estimation (or classification) stage. However, some preprocessing needs to be carried out to determine the local density at $\underline{x}_i(i = 1,\ldots,n)$. This, of course, need only be done once.

The first published paper dealing with this modification to the basic kernel estimator seems to be that of Wagner (1975). This is a theoretically oriented paper showing various convergence results for the variable kernel estimator. We discussed various types of convergence in Section 2.2 and here present Wagner's results. Note that Wagner considers the unidimensional case, but comments that extension to an arbitrary number of variables is straightforward.

Theorem 3.6.1: (Wagner, 1975) With the Rosenblatt kernel, if $h = h(x_1,\ldots,x_n)$ is a symmetric function of $x_1,\ldots,x_n$ and if

(i) $h \rightarrow 0$ in probability

(ii) $n^\alpha h \rightarrow \infty$ in probability for $0 < \alpha < \frac{1}{2}$ then $\hat{f}(x) \rightarrow f(x)$ in probability at each x for which f is continuous.

The phrase "in probability" in Theorem 3.6.1 can be replaced everywhere by the phrase "with probability one" and the resulting new theorem is also true. Furthermore, if in addition f is uniformly continuous on R then the same results (in probability, with probability

118

one) show that $\sup_x |\hat{f}(x)-f(x)| \to 0$ (in probability, with probability one).

We now have to find an h satisfying (i) and (ii) of theorem 3.6.1.

Theorem 3.6.2: (Wagner, 1975) Let $k(n) = \{n^\beta\}$ with $0 < \beta < 1$ and let D_{-jn} be the distance from x_j to its $k(n)$th nearest neighbour in the design set $\{x_1,...,x_n\}$ with x_j omitted (j = 1,...,n). Select h at random from D_{1n} to D_{nn}. Then

(i) $h \to 0$ in probability

(ii) $n^\alpha h \to \infty$ in probability if $1-\beta < \alpha$.

Of particular relevance to the practical implementations which are discussed below is Wagner's comment that Theorem 3.6.2 remains true for

$$h = (\sum_i D_{jn})/n$$

or

$$h = \max_j D_{jn}$$

or

$$h = \min_j D_{jn}$$

Finally, as a generalisation of Theorem 3.6.1 Wagner proves:

Theorem 3.6.3: (Wagner, 1975) If K is of bounded variation, if $\lim_{|x|\to\infty} x K(x) = 0$, and if

(i) $h \to 0$ in probability

(ii) $n^\alpha h \to \infty$ in probability for some $0 < \alpha < \frac{1}{2}$

then $\hat{f}(x) \to f(x)$ in probability for each x at which f is continuous.

Breiman, Meisel, and Purcell (1977) seem to have been the first to publish a practical application of the variable kernel method. Their spread parameter for design set point $\underline{x}_j$ is

$$h_j = \alpha d_j$$

where α is a constant multiplier and d_j is the distance from $\underline{x}_j$ to its kth nearest neighbour (omitting $\underline{x}_j$ itself) in the design set. Thus two parameters need to be determined: α and k. In their comparisons of the variable and fixed kernel estimators Breiman et al used criterion (3.3.1) to determine α, k, and h, and they used criteria (3.3.2), (3.3.3), and (3.3.4) to assess the relative performance of the two data sets, one consisting of 400 points from a bivariate normal population with identity covariance matrix and the other consisting of 400 points from a mixture of two normals, namely

$$f(\underline{x}) = \tfrac{3}{4} f_{(1)}(\underline{x}) + \tfrac{1}{4} f_{(2)}(\underline{x})$$

with

$$f_{(1)}(\underline{x}) = N((0,0),\underline{I})$$

and

$$f_{(2)}(\underline{x}) = N((3,3),\underline{I}/9)$$

In both cases the kernel was a product of standardised normal densities.

Breiman et al found that the best variable kernel estimator was always superior to the best fixed kernel estimator. The error criteria (3.3.2) and (3.3.4) were about twice as large for the fixed kernel estimator as for the variable kernel estimator, and criterion (3.3.3) was about half as big again for the fixed kernel estimator. They also noted the interesting point that the estimated optimum parameter for the fixed kernel method was much more sensitive to the error criterion chosen than was the estimated parameter for the variable kernel method - perhaps not surprisingly as a similar property holds true for k-nearest neighbour density estimates (Section 7.3). Recall also the remarks above, from Wagner (1975) about Theorem 3.6.2 being true for various choices of h.

Raatgever and Duin (1978) used the same error measures as Breiman et al (1977) and also used the Kolmogorov variational distance (3.3.5). As we have already remarked, (3.3.2), (3.3.3) and (3.3.4) only compare $f(x)$ and $\hat{f}(x)$ at the design set points whereas (3.3.5) compares the estimates at all $\underline{x}$ (and is, accordingly, a more computationally demanding criterion. Raatgever and Duin perform the integration by Monte Carlo methods). These authors also compared the estimation criterion (3.3.1) used by Breiman et al (1977) with the modified maximum likelihood method (Section 3.4). Their data came from normal and lognormal distributions with sample sizes from 10 to 100. For normal distributions not much difference was found between the parameter estimation methods and not much difference in performance was found between the fixed and variable kernel methods. For lognormal distributions again the two parameter estimation methods gave broadly similar results but now the variable kernel method did substantially better than the fixed kernel method.

Habbema, Hermans and Remme (1978) compared fixed and variable kernel methods using a criterion measuring the accuracy of the estimate of posterior probabilities (described in Section 3.5) by weighting small disagreements between $\hat{\pi}_i \, \hat{f}_i(\underline{x})$ and $\pi_i \, f_i(\underline{x})$ by one unit and large disagreements by ten units. They performed simulations on data from two multivariate normal classes (with both equal and unequal covariance matrices), lognormal classes, and classes with normal mixture distributions. The results were in accordance with those reported above: no pronounced optimum for k and the variable kernel method was markedly superior for the lognormal case but in other cases there was no clear superiority either way. They also applied the method to a sample of real data, where the aim was to discriminate between two kinds of hypercalcaemia, and found that the variable kernel method gave better results (investigation revealed the data to be skew).

To summarise, it seems that the variable kernel method should be used rather than the fixed kernel method. The former never performs substantially worse than the latter and can perform markedly better - especially if the class conditional distributions are skew. (Or if $f'(\underline{x})$ varies a lot?) Since without extensive data analysis we will normally know little about the distribution of the data it obviously makes sense to choose the variable kernel method.

There is another way of handling skew distributions for the univariate case, though modifying it for application to the multivariate cases which characteristically confront us in classification problems may be difficult. This is simply to transform the sample distribution prior to carrying out the estimation and then transforming back (Ojo, 1974; Copas and Fryer, 1980).

CHAPTER 4
Categorical Variables

4.1   INTRODUCTION

Discrimination and pattern recognition techniques for use on categorical variables are becoming increasingly important. This is partly a consequence of the recognition of the inappropriateness of classical continuous variable techniques to such problems and partly a consequence of the growth in applications of pattern recognition methods to problem areas where categorical variables are common. Such areas include the behavioural sciences (such as sociology, psychology, and psychiatry) where categorical variables are the norm rather than the exception, and medicine. In view of their prevalence, however, it is not surprising that standard pattern recognition methods, with their implicit assumptions of at least interval scale continuous data, have been applied to these problems. In particular the classical Fisher linear discriminant function method (Lachenbruch, 1975; Hand,1981b) has been so applied. In fact, at the time of writing, due to its position as the most widely implemented statistical discriminant analysis algorithm, it seems fair to say that Fisher's method is still the method most widely used on categorical data. Recognising this, some authors (e.g. Gilbert, 1968; Moore, 1973; Krzanowski, 1977) have studied the performance of this classical method on categorical variables. Clearly this is not the place to dwell on such studies. Suffice it to say that the results can usually be predicted fairly well on a priori theoretical grounds: if the data are known to come from distributions suited to the continuous variable method, then the latter gives acceptable results. Of course, this leaves open the question of how the methods perform on real data.

Recently, however, methods specially designed for categorical variables have been developed. Some of these methods are described in Goldstein and Dillon (1978) and a more global though less detailed summary is given in Hand (1981a). A quick glance at some of these will indicate the motivation behind the development of the categorical variable kernel method.

First let us consider the most obvious estimator for distributions over categorical variables, the multinomial estimator. Here the class conditional probability in a cell $\underline{x}$ (where $\underline{x}$ is a vector whose components can take only a finite number of values - usually a small number) is estimated by the proportion of design set points falling within that cell. Thus if $n(\underline{x})$ of the n design set points (for this class) fall in cell $\underline{x}$ the multinomial estimator is

$$r(\underline{x}) = n(\underline{x})/n \ .$$

This estimator has a number of extremely desirable properties. It is the minimum variance unbiased estimator, it is straightforward and easy to implement and interpret, and it is the maximum likelihood estimator. However, it has one extremely undesirable property - a property which is demonstrated when we come to apply the method in practice. Later in this chapter we consider part of the data used for designing a questionnaire to detect individuals who have a high risk of suffering from psychiatric illness. The complete questionnaire consists of 30 questions, coded as binary variables. The aim is to classify people as high or low risk on the basis of their 30 responses. Suppose that, for reliable estimates, we decided we needed an average of ten design set observations per cell for each class. Since there are two classes and 2^{30} cells this means that we need 2^{31} x 10 design set points. That is, about 10^{10} such points. Since here each point consists of the responses to 30 questions plus a classification derived from a psychiatric interview we need to interview more people than there are currently alive on earth - just to design the classifier. The alternative is that many of our future classifications will be made by comparing a probability estimate of 0 with another one of 0. Clearly this is not a very satisfactory state of affairs.

This is not intended to give the impression that the multinomial estimator can never be used. If the total number of cells, G, is small enough and the design set is big enough, then such an approach may be perfectly feasible. But note that difficulties can arise even if the ratio n/G is not small when $p(\underline{x})$ (the probability that an observation from this class will fall in cell $\underline{x}$) is small for some $\underline{x}$.

The basic problem has arisen, of course, because there are $G = \prod\limits_{i=1}^{d} g_i$ parameters (where g_i is the number of categories in the ith variable) to be estimated but there is insufficient data to do this.

Other approaches for categorical data can be suggested by analogy with the continuous variable case. In such a situation we need in principle an infinite number of parameters to describe the class conditional distribution $f_i(\underline{x})$. This impossible situation is often tackled by assuming <u>a priori</u> that the class conditional distributions belong to some family (that they are normal, for example) and identifying the particular members of the family by estimating the (small) finite number of parameters. To follow this sort of approach with categorical data we abandon the hope of estimating all G parameters (for each class) and instead assume that the class conditional distributions belong to some family, indexed by M < G parameters. Rather than adopting an arbitrary family without justification, however, the usual approach is to reparameterise the distribution so that the G new parameters do not have the symmetry of the multinomial $p(\underline{x})$. This lack of symmetry can then be exploited to reduce the number of parameters. Thus, for example, if n/G is not small log-linear model building processes apply model fitting tests to eliminate high order interactions - but if n/G is small it may be necessary to <u>assume</u> from the start that some of these interactions are zero. Latent class models, on the other hand, assume that the distribution of each class is a mixture of a small number of constituent distributions and that within each of these distributions the variables are independent. Thus right from the start M < G.

Of course, it is possible that one is loath to make such assumptions, feeling that they may be an imposition of structure on the data rather than a reflection of structure within it.

So, given that there is not enough data to estimate G independent parameters and given that one may feel uneasy about assuming an arbitrary class of structures, what alternatives are there? Several authors, including Good (1965), Fienberg and Holland (1973), Stone

(1974a) and Titterington (1980) have considered estimators of the general form

$$\hat{p}(\underline{x}) = (1-\alpha) \frac{n(x)}{n} + \alpha \; m(\underline{x}) \qquad (4.1.1)$$

where $0 \leq \alpha \leq 1$. Estimators of this form can be derived by both Bayesian and non-Bayesian arguments and interest has been particularly focussed on the choice $m(\underline{x}) \equiv 1/G$. Study of (4.1.1) rveals that it is a linear combination of the crude multinomial estimator $n(\underline{x})/n$ and the function $m(\underline{x})$. The smaller α is, the more closely $\hat{p}(\underline{x})$ resembles $n(\underline{x})/n$. The larger α is, the more closely $\hat{p}(\underline{x})$ resembles $m(\underline{x})$. In a Bayesian interpretation α would be regarded as a measure of the relative importance of the data and prior knowledge. (See Bishop, Fienberg and Holland, 1975, Chapter 12 for an extensive discussion of this.)

Usually $m(\underline{x})$ in (4.1.1) will be specified independently of the data. However, sometimes models of the form (4.1.1) are used in which $m(\underline{x})$ depends on the design set distribution. This is true of categorical data kernel estimates. Rather than introducing them in this way we shall adopt a different approach in the next section and then point out how they may be rewritten to be like (4.1.1). Before progressing to the next section note that: $\hat{p}(\underline{x})$ in (4.1.1) is essentially a combination of the ultimate local estimator $n(\underline{x})/n$ and a particular global model $m(\underline{x})$; there is a single parameter, α, to be determined; and if $m(\underline{x})$ is appropriately chosen $\hat{p}(\underline{x}) \neq 0$ for all $\underline{x}$. By letting the data play some role in determining $m(\underline{x})$ we relax the arbitrariness associated with specifying the global model.

From the above discussion of multinomial and parametric approaches it is clear that estimators of the form (4.1.1), and in particular kernel estimators, might sometimes be preferred to other approaches.

4.2   KERNELS FOR CATEGORICAL VARIABLES

As with the continuous variable case, the kernel method with categorical data estimates the probability at a point $\underline{x}$ by an average of contributions from the design set elements:

$$\hat{p}(\underline{x}) = \frac{1}{n} \sum_{i=1}^{n} K(\underline{x},\underline{x}_i)$$

And, as before, the kernel K is a function of a distance measure between $\underline{x}$ and $\underline{x}_i$, inversely monotonically related to this distance, so that $\underline{x}_i$ points near $\underline{x}$ contribute more to $\hat{p}(\underline{x})$ than $\underline{x}_i$ points far from $\underline{x}$. Although there has been less work on the choice of kernel function in the categorical variable case than in the continuous variable case a number of choices have been suggested.

Perhaps the first, and certainly the simplest particular form, was suggested by Hills (1967). Here

$$K(\underline{x},\underline{x}_i) = \begin{array}{l} 1 \text{ if } D(\underline{x},\underline{x}_i) < t \\ 0 \text{ otherwise} \end{array} \qquad (4.2.1)$$

where t is a threshold and $D(\underline{x},\underline{x}_i)$ is a measure of the distance between $\underline{x}$ and $\underline{x}_i$. Hills used Euclidean distance

$$D(\underline{x},\underline{x}_i) = (\underline{x} - \underline{x}_i)'(\underline{x} - \underline{x}_i)$$

In fact Hills refers to this method as a nearest neighbour method but in keeping with current nomenclature it is more accurate to describe it as a kernel method. Kernel (4.2.1) is directly analogous to the Rosenblatt kernel (2.1.1), giving an identical contribution from design set points falling within a distance t of $\underline{x}$ and a zero contribution from other points. Although it has the merit of being simple, it does suffer from some disadvantages: zero estimates can still result, it is not necessarily consistent, and it is difficult to justify the fact that a point $\underline{x}_i$ just within the threshold distance contributes to $\hat{p}(\underline{x})$ while one just outside the threshold does not. Note, of course that, with t less than the minimum distance between cells the straightforward estimate $\hat{p}(\underline{x}) = n(\underline{x})/n$ results.

The Hills kernel is an explicit discrete variable analogue for the Rosenblatt continuous variable kernel. Wang and Van Ryzin (1981) present an explicit discrete variable analogue for more general univariate Parzen continuous variable kernels. We shall adopt the notation $K(x,y,h)$ to represent the kernel centred at x and with smoothing parameter h. Whereas before x and y were continuous variables, now they are categorical. That is $x.y \in \{...,-1,0,1,...\}$. h is chosen from a specified interval S of R. The kernel estimator of $p(x)$ is

$$\hat{p}(x) = \frac{1}{n} \sum_{j=1}^{n} K(x,y_j,h)$$

where y_j is the jth design set element (for this class).

Wang and Van Ryzin make the restrictions, discussed at some length for continuous variables in Chapters 2 and 3, that

$$\sum_{y=-\infty}^{\infty} K(x,y,h) = 1$$

and $K(x,y,h) >= 0$ for all $x,y \in \{...,-1,0,1...\}$ and $h \in S$. They also require that

$$K(x,y,0) = \begin{matrix} 0 & x \neq y \\ 1 & x = y \end{matrix}$$

corresponding to the continuous variable delta function when h = 0.

The authors then go on to derive optimal forms for h (as we show in Section 4.3.4), in which h is a function of the unknown true probabilities $p(\underline{x})$. The following theorem, which they prove, then permits us to substitute the maximum likelihood estimate $n(\underline{x})/n$ for p($\underline{x}$) in the expressions for the optimal h, giving estimates $\hat{h}$ for h.

Theoreom 4.2.1: (Wang and Van Ryzin, 1981). Let K be as described above and let $P(\hat{h} \ \epsilon \ S) = 1$.

(a) If $\hat{h} \to 0$ in probability then

$$\frac{1}{n} \sum_{j=1}^{n} K(x,y_j,\hat{h}) \to p(x)$$

in probability as $n \to \infty$.

(b) If $\hat{h}\sqrt{n} \to 0$ in probability as $n \to \infty$ and if $K(x,y,h)$ has a continuous first derivative at 0 then

$$\{\frac{1}{n} \sum_{j=1}^{n} K(x,y_j,\hat{h}) - p(x)\}\sqrt{n}$$

converges in distribution to a normal random variable with mean 0 and variance $p(x)\{1-p(x)\}$.

Furthermore, if the convergence in (a) is with probability 1 then the conclusion is with probability 1.

As a corollary to this they present:

Theorem 4.2.2: (Wang and Van Ryzin, 1981). If K is as described above then (a) and (b) of the preceding theorem hold for the kernel estimator $\hat{p}(x)$ when h is nonrandom if $\lim h\sqrt{n} = 0$.

Wang and Van Ryzin illustrate with two particular kernel forms:

(i) The uniform kernel

$$
K(x,y,h) = \begin{cases} \dfrac{h}{2k} & |x-y| = 1,\dots,k \text{ (k a fixed integer} >=1) \\ 1-h & x=y \\ 0 & |x-y| > k \end{cases} \tag{4.2.2}
$$

with $h \ \epsilon \ (0,1)$.

(ii)   The geometric kernel

$$K(x,y,h) = \tfrac{1}{2}(1-h)h^{|x-y|} \qquad \frac{|x-y| \geq 1}{x=y} \qquad (4.2.3)$$

with $h \in (0,1)$.

An alternative kernel form - and one which is currently probably the most widely used in practical applications - has been suggested by Aitchison and Aitken (1976). Rather than introducing it in a form suitable for general categorical variables, however, it will considerably ease the exposition if we first outline it for binary variables. We shall begin with a single variable and generalise.

With a single binary variable it is apparent that the continuous variable kernels become simply two numbers, one for the situation when $|x-y| = 0$ and one for the situation when $|x-y| = 1$. Calling these numbers a and b respectively, the monotonicity requirement (i.e. that a point far from x contributes less to $\hat{p}(x)$) implies a >= b. Thus a general form for the univariate binary kernel is

$$K_j(x,y) = \begin{cases} a \text{ if } (\underline{x}-\underline{y})'(\underline{x}-\underline{y}) = 0 \\[2mm] b \text{ if } (\underline{x}-\underline{y})'(\underline{x}-\underline{y}) = 1 \end{cases}$$

where a >= b.

The multivariate product kernel is then defined as a product of these univariate kernels

$$K(\underline{x},\underline{y}) = \prod_{j=1}^{d} K_j(x_j,y_j) \qquad (4.2.4)$$

Aitchison and Aitken in fact use a and b of the form

$$a = \lambda \qquad b = 1-\lambda \qquad \tfrac{1}{2} \leq \lambda \leq 1$$

so that (4.2.4) may be expressed as

$$K(\underline{x},\underline{y}) = \prod_{j=1}^{d} \lambda^{1-|x_j-y_j|}(1-\lambda)^{|x_j-y_j|} \qquad (4.2.5)$$

or, equivalently

$$K(\underline{x},\underline{y}) = \lambda^{d-D(\underline{x},\underline{y})} (1-\lambda)^{D(\underline{x},\underline{y})} \qquad (4.2.6)$$

where

$$D(\underline{x},\underline{y}) = (\underline{x}-\underline{y})'(\underline{x}-\underline{y}) = \sum_{j=1}^{d} (x_j-y_j)^2 = \sum_{j=1}^{d} |x_j-y_j|$$

is the number of variables on which binary vectors $\underline{x}$ and $\underline{y}$ differ. When $\frac{1}{2} <= \lambda <= 1$ we have

$$\lambda^d >= \lambda^{d-1}(1-\lambda) >= \lambda^{d-2}(1-\lambda)^2 >= \ldots >= (1-\lambda)^d$$

so that the required monotonicity condition is satisfied for all d.

Note that since (4.2.5) is directly analogous to the product kernels of Chapter 3 we can use different K_j in (4.2.4). That is, different λ's in (4.2.5) as

$$K(\underline{x},\underline{y}) = \prod_{j=1}^{d} \lambda_j^{1-|x_j-y_j|} (1-\lambda_j)^{|x_j-y_j|} \qquad (4.2.7)$$

Whether the additional complexity of having d parameters instead of 1 can be justified remains to be seen. Note that, while a single smoothing parameter may be appropriate for continuous variables after normalising them by dividing by their standard deviations, such standardisation is not practicable for binary variables.

We have, in Chapters 2 and 3, discussed at some length the merits and demerits of requiring $\int K(\underline{x})d\underline{x} = 1$ for continuous variables. From the form of (4.2.6) it is easy to see that there are:

$\binom{d}{0}$ = 1 cells which contribute a term λ^d

$\binom{d}{1}$ = d cells which contribute a term $\lambda^{d-1}(1-\lambda)$

$\binom{d}{2}$ = $\dfrac{d(d-1)}{2}$ cells which contribute a term $\lambda^{d-2}(1-\lambda)^2$

. . . .

$\binom{d}{d} = 1$ cells which contribute a term $(1-\lambda)^d$.

This is simply a binomial expansion of $\{(1-\lambda) + \lambda\}^d$ so that

$$\sum_{\underline{y}} K(\underline{x},\underline{y}) = \{(1-\lambda) + \lambda\}^d = 1$$

where the summation is over all 2^d cells in the binary space.

Finally, note that (4.2.6) can be written in the equivalent form

$$K(\underline{x},\underline{y}) = \lambda^d \{(1-\lambda)/\lambda\}^{D(\underline{x},\underline{y})}$$

$$= \lambda^d \, \alpha^{D(\underline{x},\underline{y})} \tag{4.2.8}$$

where $\alpha = (1-\lambda)/\lambda$. The monotonicity condition will then be satisfied if $0 <= \alpha <= 1$. This form will ease computation. For example, a two class classification rule

$$\frac{1}{n_1} \sum_{i=1}^{n_1} \lambda_1^d \alpha_1^{D(\underline{x},\underline{x}_i)} / \frac{1}{n_2} \sum_{i=1}^{n_2} \lambda_2^d \alpha_2^{D(\underline{x},\underline{y}_i)} \gtrless k_A \to \underline{x} \in \begin{array}{l} \text{class 1} \\ \text{class 2} \end{array}$$

becomes

$$\sum_{i=1}^{n_1} \alpha_1^{D(\underline{x},\underline{x}_i)} / \sum_{i=1}^{n_2} \alpha_2^{D(\underline{x},\underline{y}_i)} \gtrless k_B \to \underline{x} \in \begin{array}{l} \text{class 1} \\ \text{class 2} \end{array} \tag{(4.2.9)}$$

To extend the method to general nominal variables, which have no intrinsic ordering between the g_j categories for variable j, we can use in place of

$$K_j(x,y) = \begin{array}{l} \lambda_j \text{ if } x = y \\ \\ 1-\lambda_j \text{ if } x \neq y \end{array} \qquad \text{(x,y binary)}$$

the more general form

$$K_j(x,y) = \begin{array}{l} \lambda_j \text{ if } x = y \\ \\ \dfrac{1-\lambda_j}{g_j-1} \text{ if } x \neq y \end{array} \tag{4.2.10}$$

Binary variables are the special case of $g_j = 2$. Note that (4.2.10) preserves the unit sum condition. That is,

$$\sum_{\underline{y}} K(\underline{x},\underline{y}) = \sum_{\underline{y}} \prod_{j=1}^{d} K_j(x_j,y_j) = 1 \qquad (4.2.11)$$

Ordinal variables present greater difficulty. As described above the choice of kernel is an implicit choice of a distance function so that it seems to imply an underlying assumption of an interval scale. While it might be possible to reformulate the kernel method, or simply to view it from a more general position which encompasses ordinal variables, we have as yet seen no adequate treatment. Nevertheless, for interest we present the kernel suggested by Aitchison and Aitken (1976) for the three category ordinal variable case. This kernel preserves the condition given in (4.2.11). If x_j and y_j are the jth components of $\underline{x}$ and $\underline{y}$ then $K_j(x_j,y_j)$ is given by the following, where x_j and y_j can take the values 0,1, or 2:

	$y_j = 0$	1	2
$x_j = 0$	λ^2	$2\lambda(1-\lambda)$	$(1-\lambda)^2$
1	$\frac{1}{2}(1-\lambda^2)$	λ^2	$\frac{1}{2}(1-\lambda^2)$
2	$(1-\lambda)^2$	$2\lambda(1-\lambda)$	λ^2

Other kernel forms have been suggested. Titterington (1980), for example, lets

$$\hat{p}(\underline{x}) = \underline{C}'\underline{r}$$

where $\underline{C}$ is a G x G matrix of non-negative elements such that

$$\sum_i C_{ij} = \sum_j C_{ij} = 1 \text{ for all } i,j = 1,..,G$$

and where $\underline{r}$ is the column vector with ith element the proportion of design set points in the ith cell. Titterington suggests that $\underline{C}$ is taken to be

$$\underline{C} = \underline{I} + (1-\lambda)\underline{D}$$

where
$$D_{ii} = -1 \qquad i = 1,\ldots,G$$
$$\underline{D\ell} = 0 \qquad \underline{\ell}' = (1,1,\ldots,1)$$
$$D_{ij} \geq 0 \qquad i \neq j$$

When $C_{ii} = \lambda$ $(i = 1,\ldots,G)$ and $C_{ij} = (1-\lambda)/(G-1)$ $(i \neq j)$ we have the univariate kernel (4.2.10).

One way of handling missing data (see Section 6.4) is to treat "missing" as an extra category. With binary variables one can then treat the resulting three category variable as either unordered or ordered with "missing" between 0 and 1. Murray and Titterington (1978) suggest the following kernel form for this case of binary variables with missing data (where $\underline{x}$ refers to the point at which the estimate is being made and $\underline{y}$ refers to a design set point):

$y_j =$	0	1	missing
$x_j = 0$	λ^2	$\lambda(1-\lambda)$	$(1-\lambda)$
1	$\lambda(1-\lambda)$	λ^2	$(1-\lambda)$
missing	$(1-\lambda^2)/2$	$(1-\lambda^2)/2$	λ^2

Note that this can be expressed as

$$K_j(x_j,y_j) = \begin{cases} \lambda K_0(x_j,y_j) & \text{if both } x_j \text{ and } y_j \text{ are not missing} \\ (1-\lambda) & \text{if } x_j \text{ is missing and } y_j \text{ is not} \\ \lambda^{g_j+1} & \text{if both are missing} \\ (1-\lambda^{g_j+1})/g_j & \text{if } x_j \text{ is present and } y_j \text{ is missing.} \end{cases}$$

where $K_0(x_j,y_j)$ is the ordinary binary variable kernel for data with no missing values (and g_j is, again, the number of categories of the jth variable).

136

Yet another form has recently been considered by Hall (1981a). He considers multivariate binary data and finds the categorical equivalent of the MISE optimal form for the kernel (MISE optimal kernels for continuous variables are discussed at some length in Chapter 3). That is, he seeks to minimise

$$\sum_{\underline{x}} E\{\hat{p}(\underline{x}) - p(\underline{x})\}^2 \qquad (4.2.12)$$

by choice of weights w_j in

$$\hat{p}(\underline{x}) = \frac{1}{n} \sum_{j=0}^{t} w_j\, n_j(\underline{x})$$

where $n_j(\underline{x})$ is the number of observation points at distance j from $\underline{x}$, and t is a threshold distance. That is

$$n_j(\underline{x}) = \sum_{\{\underline{y}\,|\,(\underline{x}-\underline{y})'(\underline{x}-\underline{y})\,=\,j\}} n(\underline{y}) \qquad (4.2.13)$$

Hall shows that the weight vector $\underline{w} = (w_0,\ldots,w_t)'$ which minimises (4.2.12) is

$$\underline{w} = \{\underline{P} + n^{-1}(\underline{D} - \underline{P})\}^{-1}\underline{p} \qquad (4.2.14)$$

where

$$\underline{p} = \sum_{\underline{x}} p(\underline{x})\underline{s}(\underline{x}) \qquad (4.2.15)$$

$$\underline{s}(\underline{x}) = (p(\underline{x}),p_1(\underline{x}),\ldots,p_t(\underline{x})) \qquad (4.2.16)$$

$$p_i(\underline{x}) = \sum_{\{\underline{y}\,|\,(\underline{x}-\underline{y})'(\underline{x}-\underline{y})\,=\,i\}} p(\underline{y}) \qquad (4.2.17)$$

$$\underline{P} = \sum_{\underline{x}} \underline{s}(\underline{x})\underline{s}'(\underline{x}) \qquad (4.2.18)$$

and

$$\underline{D} = \text{diag}\{\tbinom{d}{0},\tbinom{d}{1},\ldots,\tbinom{d}{t}\}. \qquad (4.2.19)$$

(4.2.14) can be rewritten as

$$\underline{w} = \{(1 - n^{-1})\underline{I} + n^{-1}\underline{P}^{-1}\underline{D}\}^{-1}\underline{i}$$

$$= (1 + n^{-1})\underline{i} - n^{-1}\underline{P}^{-1}\underline{Di} + 0(n^{-2})$$

using $\underline{i} = (1,0,\ldots,0)'$, a $(t+1)$ component vector. Maximum likelihood estimates $n(\underline{x})/n$ for the $p(\underline{x})$ are then substituted to lead, via (4.2.15-19), to $\hat{\underline{P}}$ and $\hat{\underline{D}}$ and hence to the estimator

$$\hat{\underline{w}}_1 = \{(1-n^{-1})\underline{I} + n^{-1}\hat{\underline{P}}^{-1}\hat{\underline{D}}\}^{-1}\underline{i} \qquad (4.2.20)$$

Alternatively, the second simpler form for $\underline{w}$ above could be used to give

$$\hat{\underline{w}}_1^* = (1+n^{-1})\underline{i} - n^{-1}\hat{\underline{P}}^{-1}\hat{\underline{Di}} \qquad (4.2.21)$$

Hall points out that the resulting estimates may not sum to unity and modifies the weights so that this condition is satisfied by minimising (4.2.12) subject to $\underline{w}'\underline{h} = 1$ using Lagrange multipliers and

$$\underline{h} = (\tbinom{d}{0}, \tbinom{d}{1}, \ldots, \tbinom{d}{t}))'.$$

This gives

$$\hat{\underline{w}}_2 = \hat{\underline{w}}_1 + \hat{\underline{B}}^{-1}\underline{\ell}(1-\underline{h}'\hat{\underline{B}}^{-1}\underline{i})/(\underline{h}'\hat{\underline{B}}^{-1}\underline{\ell}) \qquad (4.2.22)$$

where $\hat{\underline{B}} = (1-n^{-1})\underline{I} + n^{-1}\hat{\underline{P}}^{-1}\hat{\underline{D}}$ and $\underline{\ell}$ is the $(t+1)$ component vector of 1's.

The estimates can be negative - though as we have already pointed out this may not be a disadvantage since comparisons and hence classifications can still be made. They are also slightly biased. If $\underline{w}_1$ is of the form (4.2.20) with estimates $\hat{\underline{P}}$ and $\hat{\underline{D}}$ replaced by their true values and if $\underline{w}_2$ is of the form (4.2.22) with $\hat{\underline{B}}$ replaced by its true value then Hall states that

$$\hat{\underline{w}}_1 - \underline{w}_1, \ \hat{\underline{w}}_2 - \underline{w}_2 = \begin{cases} 0(n^{-3/2}) \text{ in probability} \\ \\ 0(n^{-3}\log\log n) \text{ almost surely.} \end{cases}$$

As we have noted before an obvious iterative technique is to repeat the above evaluation of $\hat{\underline{w}}_1$ and $\hat{\underline{w}}_2$ with the new estimated $\hat{p}(\underline{x})$ replacing the maximum likelihood estimates $n(\underline{x})/n$.

It should be noted that the above results clearly require $\underline{P}$ to be non-singular. Hall does briefly discuss the case when $\underline{P}$ is singular, but points out that this is not a likely occurrence.

To test his alternative form of kernel, Hall compared it with those of Aitchison and Aitken (1976) and Hills (1967). The estimators $\hat{\underline{w}}_1$ and $\hat{\underline{w}}_2$ above gave very similar results, and these were very similar to those produced by Aitchison and Aitken's method - but differed from Hills's results. Wang and Van Ryzin (1981) have also compared a number of different kernel functions for the case of univariate discrete distributions. Their conclusion (p.309): "From Table 2 and the numerical results for other weight functions, it appears that the choice of the weight function has little effect to (sic) the performance of a discrete density estimate." This conforms to most (but not all) of the continuous variable results. Wang and Van Ryzin recommend the use of the uniform kernel (4.2.2) with k = 1 or 2 on the grounds that these are simple and that the optimal h based on these are exact (see Section 4.3.4).

4.3   CHOOSING SMOOTHING PARAMETERS

In this section we focus attention chiefly on product kernels with factors of the form (4.2.10) since most published work deals with this form. We will briefly describe more general situations. As with continuous data, there are many bases on which the spread parameters may be chosen and many ways through which the choice may be made.

First, since we are dealing with multivariate data, there is the fundamental choice of whether we should have different parameters for each dimension or a single common parameter. That is, should we restrict $\lambda_i = \lambda_j = \lambda$ for all i, j = 1,...,d? Secondly, should we choose the parameters by overall global multivariate considerations, or can we consider each marginal separately? (If there is to be a single λ, the same for each dimension, we could estimate separate parameters for each marginal and then use some kind of average.) If the λ_i are not constrained to be equal one might expect marginal methods to give larger λ_i's (sharper estimated distributions) than the true multivariate methods. Titterington (1980) found this to be the case.

4.3.1   Maximum Likelihood

Here the λ_j are chosen by maximising

$$J_1(\underline{\lambda}) = \prod_{j=1}^{n} \hat{p}(\underline{x}_j) \qquad (4.3.1)$$

Aitchison and Aitken (1976) give an elegant and brief demonstration that the maximising λ_j are $\lambda_j = 1$. First note that (4.3.1) may be rewritten as

$$J_1(\underline{\lambda}) = \prod_{\underline{x}\ \underline{y}}\{\Sigma r(\underline{y})K(\underline{x},\underline{y}|\underline{\lambda})\}^{n(\underline{x})}$$

where the subscripts $\underline{x}$ and $\underline{y}$ indicate that the range is all G cells and where $r(\underline{y}) = n(\underline{y})/n$ is the proportion of design set points in cell $\underline{y}$. $K(\underline{x},\underline{y}|\underline{\lambda})$ is

$$K(\underline{x},\underline{y}|\underline{\lambda}) = \prod_{j=1}^{d} K_j(x_j,y_j|\lambda_j)$$

with K_j as in (4.2.10). Taking the logarithm of $J_1(\underline{\lambda})$ then yields, with $\underline{\ell} = (1,1,...,1)'$;

140

$$\{\log J_1(\underline{\ell})-\log J_1(\underline{\lambda})\}/n = \Sigma r(\underline{x})\log \frac{\Sigma r(\underline{y})K(\underline{x},\underline{y}|\underline{\ell})}{\Sigma\, r(\underline{y})K(\underline{x},\underline{y}|\underline{\lambda})}$$

However, since $K(\underline{x},\underline{y}|\underline{\ell}) = 1$ if and only if $\underline{x} = \underline{y}$ and is zero otherwise we have

$$\{\log J_1(\underline{\ell}) - \log J_1(\underline{\lambda})\}/n = \Sigma r(\underline{x})\log \frac{r(x)}{\Sigma r(\underline{y})K(\underline{x},\underline{y}|\underline{\lambda})}$$

which is positive unless $\Sigma\, r(\underline{y})K(\underline{x},\underline{y}|\underline{\lambda}) = r(\underline{x})$, in which case it is zero. Thus $\log J_1(\underline{\lambda})$ and also, since $\log$ is a monotonic transformation, $J_1(\underline{\lambda})$ take their maximum values when $\underline{\lambda} = \underline{\ell}$. That is, the maximum is achieved when $\hat{p}(\underline{x}) = n(\underline{x})/n$.

As we commented in Section 4.1, if the ratio of n to G is large enough this solution may be of practical value but frequently n/G will not be large enough.

4.3.2   Cross Validatory Methods

As we demonstrated in Chapter 3, in the continuous variable case the maximum likelihood approach yields $h = 0$ in a way exactly analogous to the $\lambda = 1$ of the preceding section. This difficulty motivated Habbema et al (1974) and Duin (1976) to replace the likelihood function (3.4.1) by

$$J = \prod_{i=1}^{n} f^*_{(i)}(\underline{x}_i)$$

where $f^*_{(i)}$ is the kernel estimate based on the design set of $(n-1)$ points with point $\underline{x}_i$ omitted. Aitchison and Aitken (1976) adopt this procedure for use with categorical variables. The situation is exactly analogous to that of Section 3.4 and we shall only outline it briefly. Again it is more enlightening if we formulate a general framework and show that the modified maximum likelihood method is a special case.

So, let $\delta^{(i)}(\underline{x})$ be the multinomial indicator function defined by

$$\delta^{(i)}(\underline{x}) = \begin{array}{l} 1 \text{ if } \underline{x} = \underline{x}_i \\ 0 \text{ otherwise} \end{array}$$

Following Stone (1974) we define the <u>cross-validatory choice</u> of $\underline{\lambda}$ as being that value which minimises

$$J(\underline{\lambda}) = \frac{1}{n} \sum_{i=1}^{n} L \{\underline{\delta}^{(i)}, \underline{p}^*_{(i)}\} \tag{4.3.2}$$

where L is an arbitrary loss function measuring the distance between the vector with components $\delta^{(i)}(\underline{x})$ and the vector with components $p^*_{(i)}(\underline{x})$, $\underline{x}$ ranging over all G cells. Here

$$p^*_{(i)}(\underline{x}) = \frac{1}{n-1} \sum_{\substack{j=1 \\ j \neq i}}^{n} K(\underline{x}, \underline{x}_j).$$

In particular we can use the Kullback-Liebler distance measure as the loss function:

$$L(\underline{a}, \underline{b}) = \sum_{j} a_j \log(a_j/b_j) \tag{4.3.3}$$

In our case this yields

$$\begin{aligned} L \{\underline{\delta}^{(i)}, \underline{p}^*_{(i)}\} &= \sum_{\underline{x}} \delta^{(i)}(\underline{x}) \log \delta^{(i)}(\underline{x})/p^*_{(i)}(\underline{x}) \\ &= k - \sum_{\underline{x}} \delta^{(i)}(\underline{x}) \log p^*_{(i)}(\underline{x}) \\ &= k - \log p^*_{(i)}(\underline{x}_i) \end{aligned}$$

where k is independent of $\underline{\lambda}$. Thus, with this choice of loss function, (4.3.2) becomes

$$J(\underline{\lambda}) = k - \frac{1}{n} \sum_{i=1}^{n} \log p^*_{(i)}(\underline{x}_i).$$

If we now make use of the monotonicity properties of negation and logarithm, minimising $J(\underline{\lambda})$ is seen to be equivalent to maximising

$$J_2 = \prod_{i=1}^{n} p^*_{(i)}(\underline{x}_i).$$

Thus the cross validatory method based on the Kullback-Liebler loss function is the same as the modified maximum likelihood method.

The advantage of expressing the modified maximum likelihood approach as a special case of a general form is that we can immediately develop alternative methods by plugging in different loss functions. For example, we can use

(i) $\qquad L\{\underline{\delta}^{(i)},\underline{p}^{*}_{(i)}\} = \sum\limits_{\underline{x}}\{\delta^{(i)}(\underline{x}) - p^{*}_{(i)}(\underline{x})\}^2$ $\qquad\qquad$ (4.3.4)

leading to

$$J_3(\underline{\lambda}) = \sum\limits_{\underline{x}}\sum\limits_{i=1}^{n} p^{*}_{(i)}(\underline{x})^2 - 2\sum\limits_{i=1}^{n} p^{*}_{(i)}(\underline{x}_i) \qquad (4.3.5)$$

(ii) $\qquad L\{\underline{\delta}^{(i)},\underline{p}^{*}_{(i)}\} = \sum\limits_{\underline{x}}\{\delta^{(i)}(\underline{x}) - p^{*}_{(i)}(\underline{x})\}^2/p^{*}_{(i)}(\underline{x})$ $\qquad$ (4.3.6)

leading to

$$J_4(\underline{\lambda}) = \sum\limits_{\underline{x}}\sum\limits_{i=1}^{n} p^{*}_{(i)}(\underline{x}) + \sum\limits_{i=1}^{n} p^{*}_{(i)}(\underline{x})^{-1} \qquad (4.3.7)$$

(iii) $\qquad L\{\underline{\delta}^{(i)},\underline{p}^{*}_{(i)}\} = \sum\limits_{\underline{x}}|\delta^{(i)}(\underline{x}) - p^{*}_{(i)}(\underline{x})|$ $\qquad\qquad$ (4.3.8)

Aitchison and Aitken (1976) consider consistency with their kernel (4.2.5) for binary variables and when λ is estimated by the above modified maximum likelihood method. They first show that the modified likelihood function has the same asymptotic form (in probability convergence terms) as the likelihood function and that for the latter, as we have shown in Section 4.3.1, the maximising λ is equal to 1. Thus $\hat{\lambda}$, the maximising λ for the modified maximum likelihood method, converges in probability to 1 as $n \to \infty$. Then, since

$$\hat{p}(\underline{x}|\underline{x}_1,\ldots,\underline{x}_n,\hat{\lambda}) = \sum\limits_{\underline{x}} \frac{n(\underline{x})}{n} K(\underline{x}|\underline{x}_i,\hat{\lambda})$$

and $n(\underline{x})/n$ converges in probability to $p(\underline{x})$ while $K(\underline{x}|\underline{x}_i,\hat{\lambda})$ converges in probability to $K(\underline{x}|\underline{x}_i,1)$, we have that as $n \to \infty$ $\hat{p}(\underline{x}|\underline{x}_1,\ldots,x_n,\hat{\lambda})$ converges in probability to

$$\sum_{\underline{x}} p(\underline{x})K(\underline{x}|\underline{x}_i,1) = p(\underline{x}).$$

(Aitchison and Aitken also point out that there are circumstances where the argument is not so straightforward.)

Bowman (1980) considers the same estimator and uses its cross validatory nature to establish consistency in the Kullback-Liebler measure. This establishes pointwise consistency.

4.3.3   Hall's Method

In Section 4.2 we described Hall's (1981a) MSE minimising kernel for multivariate binary data. Hall (1981) has applied the same criterion to estimating λ in Aitchison and Aitken type kernels, after observing that the modified maximum likelihood estimator can sometimes behave badly. He noted that if some cell is empty and all non-empty cells have more than one sample point then $\partial \log J_2(\lambda)/\partial\lambda$ can be positive at $\lambda = 1$. (J_2, here, is the modified likelihood function.) Thus $J_2(\lambda)$ can have a local maximum at $\lambda = 1$. Beginning from this observation Hall suggested, as alternative criteria, the expected sum of squares

$$J_5(\lambda) = E \sum_{\underline{x}}\{p(\underline{x}) - \hat{p}(\underline{x})\}^2 \qquad (4.3.9)$$

and a weighted expected sum of squares

$$J_6(\lambda) = \sum_{\underline{x}} p(\underline{x})E \{p(\underline{x}) - \hat{p}(\underline{x})\}^2 \qquad (4.3.10)$$

and derived expressions for $\hat{\lambda}$ based on analytic approximations.

144

Using Taylor's series to expand $\hat{p}(\underline{x})$ in powers of $(1-\lambda)$ Hall obtained

$$E\{\hat{p}(\underline{x})\} = p(\underline{x}) + (1-\lambda)\{p_1(\underline{x}) - dp(\underline{x})\} + O\{(1-\lambda)^2\}$$

and

$$nV\{\hat{p}(\underline{x})\} = p(\underline{x})\{1-p(\underline{x})\} - 2(1-\lambda)p(\underline{x})\{d(1-p(\underline{x})) +$$
$$p_1(\underline{x})\} + O\{(1-\lambda)^2\}$$

where $V(a)$ is the variance of a and $p_i(\underline{x})$ is the probability that a random observation will fall in a cell a distance i from $\underline{x}$, as in (4.2.17). By substitution in

$$E\{\hat{p}(\underline{x}) - p(\underline{x})\}^2 = V\{\hat{p}(\underline{x})\} + \{E\{\hat{p}(\underline{x})\} - p(\underline{x})\}^2$$

he obtained an expression for the mean squared error and found the $\hat{\lambda}$ which minimised it for large n, namely

$$\hat{\lambda} = 1 - p(\underline{x})\{d\{1-p(\underline{x}) + p_1(\underline{x})\}/n\{p_1(x)-dp(\underline{x})\}^2$$

One could substitute sample estimates $n(\underline{x})/n$ directly for $p(\underline{x})$ and $p_1(\underline{x})$. However, if cell $\underline{x}$ is empty then $\hat{\lambda}$ will again be 1. Moreover, $\hat{\lambda}$ as it stands is dependent on $\underline{x}$. Whilst this can be an advantage, as we have discussed in Chapter 3 for the continuous case, it is beyond the scope of the present discussion. We shall assume we require a single λ for the entire space (though, of course, possibly different ones for each class). To obtain this λ we must somehow combine the criterion measures for each $\underline{x}$ into a single global measure. An obvious candidate is the categorical variable analogue of the continuous variable mean integrated squared error, namely J_5 in (4.3.9). The λ values arising from minimising J_5 and J_6 are, respectively

$$\hat{\lambda} = 1 - \frac{d - \sum_{\underline{x}} p(\underline{x})\{p_1(\underline{x})-dp(\underline{x})\}}{n\sum_{\underline{x}}\{p_1(\underline{x}) - dp(\underline{x})\}^2} \qquad (4.3.11)$$

and

$$\hat{\lambda} = 1 - \frac{\underset{x}{\Sigma}\, p(\underline{x})^2 \{d(1 - p(\underline{x})) + p_1(\underline{x})\}}{n\underset{\underline{x}}{\Sigma}\, p(\underline{x})\{p_1(\underline{x}) - dp(\underline{x})\}^2} \qquad (4.3.12)$$

Hall suggests that $p(\underline{x})$ and $p_1(\underline{x})$ be replaced by their design set maximum likelihood estimates. An alternative is to use an iterative process

$$\hat{\lambda}_{(i)} = g\{\hat{p}(\underline{x}|\hat{\lambda}_{(i-1)})\}$$

where the function g signifies either of (4.3.11) or (4.3.12), with $\hat{\lambda}_{(i)}$ the estimate of λ at the ith iterative step and with $\hat{p}(\underline{x}|\hat{\lambda})$ the estimate at $\underline{x}$ obtained by using $\hat{\lambda}$ in the kernel estimate. $\hat{\lambda}_{(0)} = 1$ can be used as a starting value

Hall also uses criterion J_5 with second order terms in $(1-\lambda)$ included in the expansion. This yields

$$\hat{\lambda} = 1 - \frac{d + \underset{x}{\Sigma}\, p(\underline{x})\{p_1(\underline{x}) - dp(\underline{x})\}}{n\underset{\underline{x}}{\Sigma}p(\underline{x})\{2p_2(\underline{x}) + d(d+1)p(\underline{x}) - 2dp_1(\underline{x})\}} \qquad (4.3.13)$$

As before, either Hall's direct approach of substituting maximum likelihood estimates for the $p(\underline{x})$ and $p_i(\underline{x})$ or the iterative procedure suggested above can be used.

4.3.4   Marginal Approaches

We commented in Section 4.1 that (in contexts other than kernel estimation) several authors had considered replacing the crude multinomial estimate $\hat{p}(\underline{x}) = n(\underline{x})/n$ by a smoothed estimate of the form

$$\hat{p}(\underline{x}) = (1-\alpha)\frac{n(\underline{x})}{n} + \alpha m(\underline{x}) \qquad (4.3.14)$$

We could attempt to see when our more general kernel estimates on multivariate cross-classifications with G cells can be cast in this form. For example, suppose we are using the Aitchison and Aitken kernel (4.2.5) with d binary variables and with $\lambda_j = \lambda$ for $j = 1,\ldots,d$.

Then

$$\hat{p}(\underline{x}) = \frac{1}{n} \sum_{i=1}^{n} \lambda^{d-(\underline{x}-\underline{x}_i)'(\underline{x}-\underline{x}_i)} (1-\lambda)^{(\underline{x}-\underline{x}_i)'(\underline{x}-\underline{x}_i)} \tag{4.3.15}$$

$$= \sum_{\underline{y}} \frac{n(\underline{y})}{n} \lambda^{d-(\underline{x}-\underline{x}_i)'(\underline{x}-\underline{x}_i)} (1-\lambda)^{(\underline{x}-\underline{x}_i)'(\underline{x}-\underline{x}_i)}$$

$$= \frac{n(\underline{x})}{n} \lambda^d + \frac{n_1(\underline{x})}{n} \lambda^{d-1}(1-\lambda) + \frac{n_2(\underline{x})}{n} \lambda^{d-2}(1-\lambda)^2 +$$

$$\ldots \frac{n_d(\underline{x})}{n} (1-\lambda)^d,$$

where $n_i(\underline{x})$ is the number of design set points falling in cells $\underline{y}$ such that $(\underline{x}-\underline{y})'(\underline{x}-\underline{y}) = i$ (compare the $p_i(\underline{x})$ of (4.2.17)). We can rewrite this as

$$\hat{p}(\underline{x}) = \lambda^d \frac{n(\underline{x})}{n} + (1-\lambda^d)m(\underline{x})$$

where

$$m(\underline{x}) = (1-\lambda^d)^{-1}\{\frac{n_1(\underline{x})}{n}\lambda^{d-1}(1-\lambda) + \ldots + \frac{n_d(\underline{x})}{n} (1-\lambda)^d\}.$$

Thus, as we remarked but did not demonstrate in Section 4.1, kernel estimates are a special case of (4.3.14) with $\alpha = (1-\lambda^d)$. In fact this is rather contrived because $m(\underline{x})$ is a function of both α and the data. However, consider the case of a single nominal variable with g categories. Then

$$\hat{p}(x) = \lambda \frac{n(x)}{n} + \frac{(1-\lambda)}{g-1} \frac{n-n(x)}{n}$$

$$= \frac{\lambda g-1}{g-1} \frac{n(x)}{n} + \frac{1-\lambda}{g-1}$$

$$= (1-\alpha) \frac{n(x)}{n} + \frac{\alpha}{g} \tag{4.3.16}$$

where $\alpha = g(1-\lambda)/(g-1)$. This special case of (4.3.14) in particular has been the focus of attention by other authors. But how can we apply it to the multivariate situation? (The reader might care to consider why (4.3.15) in the general multivariate case did not lead to an $m(\underline{x})$ which was independent of α and the data. (This is discussed further below.) One way would be to treat the G cells of the cross-classification as comprising a single nominal variable, yielding

$$\hat{p}(\underline{x}) = \lambda\frac{n(\underline{x})}{n} + \frac{(1-\lambda)}{G-1}\frac{n-n(\underline{x})}{n}$$

but this obviously has the disadvantage of ignoring the multivariate structure - the complex ordinal interrelationships between the cells have been neglected.

An alternative is to consider the variables one at a time using (4.3.16) as a basis from which to determine a λ for each variable. As we have remarked elsewhere, if a single common λ is desired this can be obtained by an appropriate averaging process. So what alternatives exist for using (4.3.16) as a basis for λ estimates?

Stone (1974a) applies the method of cross validation (Sections 3.4 and 4.3.2) to this problem. Clearly, since in Section 4.3.2 we were discussing the general multivariate situation, what we have here is merely a special case. For the quadratic loss function (4.3.4) Stone's results lead to

$$\hat{\lambda} = \begin{cases} 1 - (1-\frac{1}{g})(\frac{n-Z}{1+(n-2)Z}) & \text{for } z \ge 1 \\ \frac{1}{g} & \text{otherwise} \end{cases} \qquad (4.3.17)$$

where

$$Z = \sum_{x}\{n(x) - n/g\}^2/\{(g-1)n/g\}.$$

With modulus loss function (4.3.8) Stone's results lead to

$$\hat{\lambda} = \begin{cases} 1 & \text{for } Z \ge 1 \\ \frac{1}{g} & \text{otherwise} \end{cases} \qquad (4.3.18)$$

Stone points out that the difference between (4.3.17) and (4.3.18) implies that $\hat{\lambda}$ is not robust to choice of loss function. He also notes that (4.3.18) is equivalent to a preliminary χ^2 test of equality of the g probabilities followed by the rule: estimate λ by the maximum likelihood estimate if the hypothesis of equality is rejected and by the assumed equal value g^{-1} if it is not. Thus if some of the cells were empty and $Z \geq 1$ (4.3.18) would lead to some zero estimates.

Bishop, Fienberg and Holland (1975) summarise their earlier work and present pseudo-Bayes methods of estimating the α in estimators of the form (4.3.16). They use the term "pseudo-Bayes" because they have the form of standard Bayes estimators except that the parameters in the priors are "estimated" from the data themselves.

Beginning with a Dirichlet distribution as prior

$$f(\underline{p}|\underline{\beta}) = \Gamma(\Sigma_x \beta(x)) \prod_x \frac{p(x)^{\beta(x)-1}}{\Gamma(\beta(x))} \qquad (4.3.19)$$

where $\beta(x) > 0$ for all x and $\Gamma(a)$ is the Gamma function (and where $\underline{p}$ signifies the vector with components $p(x)$) the posterior distribution after observing $n(x)$ design set points in cell x is again Dirichlet, now with parameters $\beta(x) + n(x)$ in place of $\beta(x)$. Things are made clearer if we reparameterise (4.3.19), putting

$$H = \Sigma_x \beta(x) \text{ and } \mu(x) = \beta(x)/H.$$

Then the prior mean of the distribution of $p(x)$ is

$$E\{p(x)|H,\underline{\mu}\} = \mu(x) \qquad (4.3.20)$$

and the posterior mean is

$$E\{p(x)|H,\underline{\mu},\underline{n}\} = \frac{n}{n+H} \frac{n(x)}{n} + \frac{H}{n+H} \mu(x) \qquad (4.3.21)$$

where $\underline{n}$ is the vector with components $n(x)$. The posterior mean is thus of form (4.3.16) with $\alpha = H/(n+H)$.

This model with a simple Dirichlet prior has been extended by Good (1967) (and is described by Bishop et al, 1975) by letting $(H,\underline{\mu})$ have a prior distribution with density function $\phi(H,\underline{\mu})$. Thus the prior for $\underline{p}$ is a mixture distribution (Everitt and Hand, 1981).

Using as risk function

$$J(\underline{\hat{p}},\underline{p}) = n\Sigma_{x} E \{\hat{p}(x) - p(x)\}^{2} \qquad (4.3.22)$$

(c.f. (4.3.9)) Bishop et al derive the risk of the maximum likelihood estimator to be

$$J(\tfrac{n}{n}n,\underline{p}) = 1 - \Sigma_{x} p(x)^{2}$$

and the risk of the estimator given by (4.3.21) to be

$$J(\underline{\hat{p}},\underline{p}) = (\tfrac{n}{n+H})^{2}\{1 - \Sigma_{x} p(x)^{2}\} + (\tfrac{H}{n+H})^{2}n\Sigma_{x}\{p(x) - \mu(x)\}^{2} \quad (4.3.23)$$

If $\underline{\mu}$ is taken as fixed - and in particular if $\mu(x) = 1/g$ for all x, as in (4.3.16) - then we can choose H by minimising $J(\underline{\hat{p}},\underline{p})$ in (4.3.23). This gives

$$H = \{1 - \Sigma_{x} p(x)^{2}\}/\{\Sigma_{x}\{p(x) - \mu(x)\}^{2}\} \qquad (4.3.24)$$

We can then estimate H by replacing p(x) by its maximum likelihood estimator n(x)/n. (c.f. the Hall approaches discussed earlier). This leads, after a little algebra, to an estimate $\hat{\alpha}$ for α (in (4.3.16)) given by

$$\hat{\alpha} = \{n^{2} - \Sigma_{x} n(x)^{2}\}/\{\Sigma_{x} n(x)^{2}(n-1) - n^{3}/g + n^{2}\} \qquad (4.3.25)$$

which in turn leads to $\hat{\lambda}$ from

$$\hat{\lambda} = 1 + \hat{\alpha}(1 - 1/g) \qquad (4.3.26)$$

Once again an iterative extension is possible.

Bishop, Fienberg and Holland (1975) use asymptotic approximations to compare the risk function (4.3.22) when p(x) is estimated on the one hand by the maximum likelihood estimator n(x)/n and on the other hand using (4.3.26). They consider two cases: $n \to \infty$ and $g \to \infty$ while maintaining n/g constant, and $n \to \infty$ with g fixed. In the first case they show that the estimator arising from (4.3.25) has a uniformly smaller risk than that arising from n(x)/n. In the second case they conclude that (4.3.25) leads to a risk which is approximately equal to that arising from n(x)/n. For small samples Bishop et al present some special cases, demonstrating that (4.3.25) leads to lower risk than the maximum likelihood approach if p is not extreme (i.e. unless $p(x) \simeq 1$ for some x). Johnson (1971) has pointed out that although the maximum likelihood estimator is an admissible estimator of p(x) with respect to (4.3.22), the reason is not because it has a uniformly small risk, but because its risk at extreme p's (i.e. those p's for which some $p(x) \simeq 1$) is small. Thus one might expect to find other estimators which have lower risk at moderate p vectors. The pseudo-Bayes estimator based on (4.3.25) is one such.

The reader should note that Bishop, Fienberg, and Holland (1975) go on to consider cross-classifications rather than single nominal variables. Again they use estimators of the form

$$\hat{p}(\underline{x}) = (1-\alpha) \frac{n(\underline{x})}{n} + \alpha m(\underline{x}).$$

Instead of taking $m(\underline{x}) = 1/G$, however, they use an m derived from the data and which takes account of the cross-classification structure. Unfortunately, if we wish to use product kernels we cannot follow this development.

Like Bishop et al and Hall (1981, 1981a), Wang and Van Ryzin (1981) have considered categorical variable equivalents of the MSE and MISE as criterion functions on which to base the estimator. As we discussed in Section 4.2, the Wang and Van Ryzin kernel is a discrete variable analogue of general Parzen univariate kernels. For some particular kernel shapes these criteria can be evaluated explicitly. The uniform kernel in (4.2.2) is one such. Using criterion

$$E_x \{\Sigma\{\hat{p}(x) - p(x)\}^2\} \qquad (4.3.27)$$

leads to

$$h = \alpha_1\{1 + 1/2k + (n-1)\alpha_2\}^{-1}$$

where

$$\alpha_1 = 1 - \sum_x p(x)^2 + A_1/2k$$

$$\alpha_2 = \sum_x p(x)^2 - A_1/k + A_0/4k^2$$

$$A_0 = \sum_x \{\sum_{|x-y|=1}^{k} p(y)^2\}$$

$$A_1 = \sum_x \{\sum_{|x-y|=1}^{k} p(x)p(y)\}$$

k a fixed integer >= 1.

Other kernel forms lead to the inclusion of higher order terms in h and approximations must be made. Wang and Van Ryzin simplify things by restricting the kernels to satisfy

$$K(x,y,h) = O\{h^{|x-y|}\}$$

so that the criteria can be written as polynomials in h plus a remainder term. That is

$$J = C_0 + C_1 h + \ldots + C_r h^r + O(h^{r+1}).$$

h is then chosen by minimising the polynomial. Wang and Van Ryzin illustrate this for the geometric kernel (4.2.3) using (4.3.27) and r = 2 to give

$$h = \beta_1 (1.5 + B_1 - B_2 + (n-1)\beta_2)^{-1}$$

where

$$\beta_1 = 1 - \sum_x p(x)^2 + B_1/2$$

$$\beta_2 = \sum_x p(x)^2 - B_1 + B_0/4$$

$$B_0 = \sum_x \{p(x-1) + p(x+1)\}^2$$

$$B_1 = \sum_x p(x)\{p(x-1) + p(x+1)\}$$

$$B_2 = \sum_x p(x)\{p(x-2) + p(x+2)\}$$

As explained in Section 4.2, the maximum likelihood estimators $n(x)/n$ are then substituted for the $p(x)$ to give strongly consistent and asymptotically normal kernel estimators. Wang and Van Ryzin also consider the lcoal mean squared error as a criterion and produce optimal smoothing parameters for both uniform and geometric kernels.

They round off their paper by large sample (theoretical derivation) and small sample (simulation) comparisons of the kernel estimators, with h given as above, against standard maximum likelihood estimators $n(x)/n$. They use a quadratic loss function and show that in both cases the kernel method is superior.

4.3.5   Other Pseudo-Bayes Methods

As with some of the authors discussed in the preceding section, Titterington (1980) also considers Bayesian methods. However, rather than taking the $p(\underline{x})$ as the parameters to be estimated and estimating λ as a means to this end, he considers the estimation of the λ to be the aim. Thus he begins (in the single binary variable case) with a Beta distribution proportional to

$$\{\frac{n(0)}{n}\lambda + \frac{n(1)}{n}(1-\lambda)\}^{n(0)}\{\frac{n(1)}{n}\lambda + \frac{n(0)}{n}(1-\lambda)\}^{n(1)}\lambda^{\beta-1}(1-\lambda)^{\gamma-1}$$

for some $\beta, \gamma > 0$. Although in principle an exact calculation could be carried out (since the posterior is a mixture of Betas) in practice this will seldom be feasible. Titterington (1980) points out that the problem can be considered as one of decomposing a mixture (Titterington, 1976; Smith and Makov, 1978; Everitt and Hand, 1981) and from this suggests the following fractional allocation method of updating the estimates of the Beta parameters:

(i) λ is assumed to follow a Beta distribution with parameters β_m, γ_m; initially $m = 0$.

(ii) At the mth stage, observation x_m is added by updating β_m and γ_m as

$$\beta_{m+1} = \beta_m + \delta_1 \; ; \; \gamma_{m+1} = \gamma_m + \delta_2$$

where

$$\delta_1 = \frac{n(0)}{n}E\{\lambda|\beta_m,\gamma_m\}/\{\frac{n(0)}{n}E\{\lambda|\beta_m,\gamma_m\} + \frac{n(1)}{n}E\{1-\lambda|\beta_m,\gamma_m\}$$
$$\delta_2 = 1-\delta_1.$$

Titterington (1980) also describes briefly the multivariate binary case with an Aitchison and Aitken type kernel assuming independent Beta priors for the λ's and demonstrating that the posterior distribution is also proportional to a product of Betas, namely

$$\prod_{i=1}^{n} K(\underline{x}_m,y_i|\lambda)^{\nu_i} \prod_{j=1}^{d} \lambda_j^{\beta_j^{(m-1)}} (1-\lambda_j)^{\gamma_j^{(m-1)}}$$

where

$$\nu_i = Q_i/\sum_{j=1}^{n} Q_j \qquad i = 1,\ldots,n$$

154

with

$$Q_i = E\{\lambda \mid \beta_i^{(m-1)}, \gamma_i^{(m-1)}\}$$

and where K is the kernel in (4.2.5).

4.4   CHOOSING A METHOD OF CHOOSING A SMOOTHING PARAMETER

In section 4.3 we presented several alternative methods for estimating the smoothing parameters for use in discrete data kernel estimates. The question thus naturally arises as to which of these methods we should use when presented with a real data set. In this section we discuss this question, concentrating primarily on the multivariate binary Aitchison and Aitken type kernel as it seems to be the form most widely used at present.

The question itself can be broken down into several parts. First, before we begin to compare methods, we should ask how critical is the choice of λ anyway. Do λ's within a large range (within $\{\frac{1}{2},1\}$, of course) provide similar results? This in turn depends how we are measuring these results: are we using misclassification rate or some more complicated loss function? Other questions then present themselves: does the choice of λ become more critical as the sample size changes? How does the n/d ratio affect things? And how about the data structure? In this section we can do no more than hint at some of the answers to some of these questions. Much more work remains to be done before definitive answers can be given.

The question of how to measure performance was discussed in some detail in Chapter 3 so we will not repeat it here. The same general principles and conclusions apply. We also, in Chapter 3, made some initial investigations into how critical was the choice of h, the continuous variable smoothing parameter. We shall give some similar comparisons on real data sets below but first let us look at other comparisons which have been made.

Hall (1981) presents an interesting paper which compares methods on grounds quite different from error rate. In fact as we have already noted in Section 4.3.3, Hall realised that the Aitchison and Aitken (1976) cross validatory method (modified maximum likelihood) could lead to zero probability estimates, with consequent difficulty of classification. Thus, if Hall's condition (some cells empty and all non-empty cells having more than one observation) occurs one might judge the modified maximum likelihood method to be poor.

Titterington (1980) has also compared estimators. For univariate binary data he performed simulations with n = 10,30, and 50 and with p(x = 1) = 0.1,0.3, and 0.5. The exact Bayesian and fractional updating methods, as described in Section 4.3.5, were run twice, with initial parameter values (β_0, γ_0) equal to (1,1) and (6,1). Table 4.1, from Titterington (1980) gives bias and MSE results for various estimators of p(x=1). Obviously, since d = 1 and g = 2 the curse of dimensionality problem does not arise and we will not obtain n(x) = 0 very often. Points about this table to note are: the maximum likelihood estimator ($\hat{\lambda}$ = 1) has smallest bias but the other estimators are usually not far behind; the good performance of other estimators as measured by root mean square is particularly striking.

Titterington (1980) has also applied twelve λ estimation methods to the keratoconjunctivitis sicca data of Anderson et al (1972). From his results Titterington notes that: (as expected) the marginal based methods tend to yield less smooth estimates than the corresponding

TABLE 4.1

Bias (with root mean square in brackets) of various estimators of p(x=1) in the single binary case (i) Maximum likelihood (ii) Kullback-Liebler cross-validatory (iii) Minimum MSE via (4.3.26) (iv) Exact Bayes with (βo,Yo) = (1,1) (v) Fractional updating with (βo,Yo) = (6,1) (vi) Exact Bayes with (βo,Yo) = (1,1) (vii) Fractional updating with (βo,Yo) = (6,1). (From Titterington, 1980).

n	p(x=1)	(i)	(ii)	(iii)	(iv)	(v)	(vi)	(vii)
10	0.1	.005 (.112)	.100 (.155)	.027 (.137)	.114 (.175)	.126 (.184)	.068 (.129)	.069 (.129)
	0.3	-.005 (.172)	.070 (.154)	.027 (.166)	.038 (.163)	.091 (.160)	.036 (.149)	.036 (.149)
	0.5	.070 (.190)	.055 (.111)	.066 (.149)	.047 (.094)	.036 (.082)	.056 (.146)	.054 (.145)
30	0.1	-.020 (.052)	.013 (.050)	-.014 (.053)	.034 (.066)	.055 (.087)	.023 (.057)	.030 (.062)
	0.3	-.020 (.061)	.025 (.070)	.007 (.065)	.060 (.088)	.106 (.121)	.024 (.058)	.030 (.058)
	0.5	.003 (.095)	.002 (.051)	-.001 (.066)	-.001 (.037)	.001 (.024)	.002 (.071)	-.003 (.071)
50	0.1	-.004 (.046)	.016 (.049)	.000 (.048)	.028 (.066)	.067 (.095)	.023 (.060)	.043 (.069)
	0.3	-.008 (.054)	.040 (.075)	.029 (.067)	.070 (.093)	.124 (.133)	.044 (.066)	.053 (.070)
	0.5	-.004 (.078)	.002 (.049)	-.001 (.057)	.003 (.037)	.002 (.019)	-.002 (.059)	-.003 (.058)

multivariate ones; the fractional updating methods "compared quite well" with the multivariate modified maximum likelihood method using different λ_j's; the minimum mean sum of squared error estimates imposed less smoothing than the modified maximum likelihood method. To study the variability caused by choice of method in practice, Titterington computed likelihood ratios for each of 41 test set patients using probability estimates derived by the various λ estimation methods. It is particularly interesting to note that the different methods led to broadly the same orderings of the likelihood ratios, suggesting perhaps that choice of method is not very critical. If this is generally true then the computationally less demanding methods should be used.

Hand (1982a) compares the Aitchison and Aitken (1976) modified maximum likelihood (cross validatory with Kullback-Liebler measure) with Hall's second order method (4.3.13) using the Aitchison and Aitken multivariate binary kernel on four real data sets (discussed further in Chapter 5). In parentheses, we might note here with reference to the concluding remark of the previous paragraph, that Hall's method requires no numerical optimisation and so is much quicker to compute. The first data set arose during a study of enuretic children. The analysis described in Hand (1982a) used 10 variables and 2 classes with a 113 point design set and a 62 point test set. (Further details of the methodology may be found in Hand, 1982a, and of the substantive enuresis issues in Dische et al, 1982). The second data set used five variables measuring patterns of psychological stress in patients in a study of general practitioner prescription patterns and had a design set of 167 points, a test set of 168 points, and 3 classes. The third data set used 12 variables from the same study. The fourth analysis involved data collected during the course of development of a mental health screening questionnaire. It had 3 classes, 8 variables and 140 points in each of the design and test sets. Table 4.2 shows the resulting λ's (different λ's for each class, the same for all variables) and the estimated misclassification rate (i.e. the proportion of the test set misclassified). In every case the Aitchison and Aitken λ estimates (A/A in the table) are smaller than the corresponding Hall estimates, sometimes surprisingly so. And yet the difference in the estimated misclassification rate is negligible. This again suggests that the choice of λ estimation method (and perhaps of λ itself) is not critical - and that the simpler estimation methods can be used without degrading the classification results. However, it should be recognised that we have implicitly made some simplifying assumptions here, as we now demonstrate.

Table 4.3 shows the misclassification table for the second (five variable) data set described above. In the particular analysis about to be described the same λ was used for each class. This is known generally to be suboptimal (but see below) but our aim here was not to find the best classifier, but merely to see how sensitive performance was to the size of spread parameter. The different rows of this table show misclassification tables for different choices of λ. Note that because of the low class 2 prior no points are allocated to this class until λ becomes quite large (i.e. the estimate becomes quite peaked). The columns in the body of the table show the losses associated with three different loss functions for the different λ's. Consider column A first. This is the traditional 0/1 loss function: a misclassification adds 1 to the loss while a correct classification

TABLE 4.2

Aitchison and Aitken versus Hall λ estimation methods used with
Aitchison and Aitken multivariate binary kernels. λ estimates and
misclassification rates are shown.

Data Set 1

	λ_1	λ_2	Misclassification Rate
A/A	0.9132	0.9155	0.323
Hall	0.9148	0.9395	0.323

Data Set 2

	λ_1	λ_2	λ_3	Misclassification Rate
A/A	0.8876	0.8622	0.8751	0.435
Hall	0.9049	0.9182	0.9103	0.435

Data Set 3

	λ_1	λ_2	λ_3	Misclassification Rate
A/A	0.8670	0.7860	0.8511	0.423
Hall	0.9347	0.9205	0.9305	0.435

Data Set 4

	λ_1	λ_2	λ_3	Misclassification Rate
A/A	0.9635	0.8796	0.8833	0.393
Hall	0.9990	0.9702	0.9859	0.393

TABLE 4.3

Losses resulting from three different loss functions using various λ's (same λ for each class) on the 5 variable psychotropic drug data.

λ	Misclassification Table				A	B	C
					0 1 1	0 1 1	0 9 1
					1 0 1	9 0 1	9 0 9
					1 1 0	9 1 0	1 9 0
		True Class					
		1	2	3			
.55	Pred. 1	0	0	0	83	587	243
	Class 2	0	0	0			
	3	63	20	85			
.60		0	0	0	83	587	243
		0	0	0			
		63	20	85			
.65		4	1	1	80	552	240
		0	0	0			
		59	19	84			
.70		16	2	7	74	450	234
		0	0	0			
		47	18	78			
.75		22	3	12	73	401	233
		0	0	0			
		41	17	73			
.80		22	4	14	75	403	235
		0	0	0			
		41	16	71			
.85		31	6	21	73	329	233
		0	0	0			
		32	14	64			
.90		34	9	23	72	304	257
		2	0	1			
		27	11	61			
.95		34	9	23	75	307	283
		3	2	5			
		26	9	57			

adds nothing. The loss values in column A are thus proportional to the misclassification rate (misclassification rate = loss/168 x 100% with this loss function and test set). It is perhaps worth noting as an aside here that if one allocated all test set points to the class with the greatest prior (class 3) one would have a loss of 83 (misclassification rate of 49%) as indicated when $\lambda = 0.55$. If one randomly allocated individuals to classes with probabilities proportional to size the loss would be 99 (misclassification rate of 59%). The major point of interest about column A is that the range of loss values for different λ is very small, and in particular any λ in the range {0.7,1.0} provides very similar results. Since this is the most commonly used loss function this point is of considerable importance and bears further investigation. Finally, note that the lowest number of misclassifications achieved is 72. If different λ's for each class are allowed and if these are estimated from the design set then the Aitchison and Aitken and Hall methods both lead to misclassifications of 73 subjects. (A slightly unfair comparison since the equal λ lowest rate was found by studying test set results in Table 4.3.)

Now consider the alternative loss function in column B. This might be applied if, for example, misclassifying class 1 points is regarded as a serious mistake (perhaps because one wishes to avoid treating patients possessing type 1 symptom profiles with antidepressants or tranquilisers - treatment with these being the defining characteristics of classes 2 and 3 respectively). Here it is seen that the range of λ values for which a small loss is achieved is much more restricted - now only {0.85, 0.95}.

Finally consider column C. This would be appropriate if class 1 to class 3 and class 3 to class 1 misclassifications were regarded as much less severe than misclassifications involving class 2. A small loss is again achieved for a fairly large range - only now the range excludes 0.95. It is apparent that the choice of loss function can have a critical effect not only on the size of range of acceptable λ values, but also on the value of the best choice.

As we note elsewhere, some authors have strongly recommended for continuous variables that different smoothing parameters should be used for each class. We therefore extended the above analysis to consider this. Specifically, we studied the variation in misclassification rates associated with using different parameters for the classes in the enuresis data and on classes 1 and 2 (ignoring class 3) in the mental health data.

Table 4.4 shows the proportions of the test set of the enuresis data misclassified at various (λ_1, λ_2) pairs. Consider the upper table first. The most striking thing about this table is that in each row and each column the smallest error rate occurs when $\lambda_1 = \lambda_2$ (i.e. the leading diagonal is a valley). In fact this is also true for the apparent error rate and the leaving-one-out error estimate leads to the best choice of (λ_1, λ_2) from the 16 pairs shown for this test set.

The reader should also compare the error rates of Table 4.4 with those for the "optimal" λ's for data set 1 in Table 4.2. These optimal λ's seem to have undersmoothed the data.

TABLE 4.4

Misclassification rates for test set of enuresis data (data set 1)
using different class 1 and class 2 smoothing parameters.

		Class 1 parameter (λ_1)			
		0.6	0.7	0.8	0.9
Class 2	0.6	0.403	0.484	0.484	0.516
Parameter	0.7	0.532	0.306	0.484	0.484
(λ_2)	0.8	0.516	0.468	0.306	0.339
	0.9	0.532	0.452	0.403	0.323

		Class 1 parameter (λ_1)			
		0.92	0.94	0.96	0.98
Class 2	0.92	0.323	0.339	0.339	0.339
Parameter	0.94	0.323	0.323	0.339	0.339
(λ_2)	0.96	0.355	0.339	0.323	0.339
	0.98	0.339	0.339	0.355	0.323

This comparison was repeated for all pairs of (λ_1, λ_2) from the set $\{0.92, 0.94, 0.96, 0.98\}$. The test set error rate is shown in the lower part of Table 4.4. Once again the smallest error rates occur down the leading diagonal. Note, however, that there is not much change in error rate over the range of λ.

Table 4.5 shows similar results for classes 1 and 2 of the mental health data. Once again the leading diagonal effect is witnessed. Note that the error rates in Table 4.5 are not comparable to those in Table 4.2 because the former uses two classes and the latter all three.

Clearly the above results are merely suggestive, both about the applicability of Aitchison and Aitken and Hall estimators for the discriminant analysis role and about the strength of the equal λ cases. Current research is directed at exploring these implications.

TABLE 4.5

Misclassification rates for the test sets of classes 1 and 2 of the mental health data (data set 4) using different smoothing parameters for each class.

		Class 1 parameter (λ_1)			
		0.92	0.94	0.96	0.98
Class 2 parameter (λ_2)	0.92	0.240	0.250	0.250	0.240
	0.94	0.263	0.240	0.250	0.240
	0.96	0.271	0.260	0.250	0.240
	0.98	0.323	0.292	0.271	0.240

CHAPTER 5
Loss Estimation and
Variable Selection

5.1   <u>INTRODUCTION</u>

In Chapters 3 and 4 we discussed at some length the choice of loss
functions to be used in estimating the smoothing parameters. As we
demonstrated, different functions lead to different estimated h's and
λ's. Thus, as we pointed out, the ideal situation would be to decide
beforehand what aspect of performance we were interested in and then
choose this aspect as the loss function. Unfortunately there are
practical difficulties associated with this ideal approach, not least
of which is the implicit fuzziness usual in these situations - it can
be impossible to decide on a rational basis quite what aspect of
performance is relevant. Thus loss functions are frequently chosen for
other reasons: for example, computational convenience, tradition, or
ease of understanding.

Here we shift the focus of our attention from the estimation of the
smoothing parameters to the assessment of discrimination performance
and to the selection of variables. Note, however, that it is but a
shift of focus. Although we will now be concerned only with
discrimination loss estimation (as opposed to loss functions which

measure accuracy of probability estimates) these functions could also be used in estimating smoothing parameters. Indeed, we considered this in earlier chapters and concluded that on balance the advantages lay with probability estimate loss functions unless it was possible to specify very precisely the aspect of classification performance with which one was concerned.

At this point it is convenient to note the role of the choice of variables in our discussion. Clearly a smoothing parameter which is optimal (as measured by some loss function) with one set of variables need not be so with another set. Thus ideally the smoothing parameters should be chosen anew - and a comparison of different sets of variables should be based on the best parameters for those sets. It will be obvious that the computational burden is beginning to increase. Because of this, for practical reasons, the selection of variables and the estimation of smoothing parameters (which stages should be performed simultaneously) are often undertaken sequentially. For example, it is common to select variables using a loss function unrelated to a kernel estimate of any kind - and then find the best parameters one can for that set of variables. One hopes that the final combination of variables and parameters is, though perhaps not optimal, at least reasonably good.

As stated above, our focus of attention here is on classification loss functions for performance assessment and variable selection. If an appropriate loss function can be chosen (for example, a physician may decide that to misclassify a person truly suffering from disease A is twice as serious as misclassifying a disease B sufferer) then well and good. In the more usual situation when the researcher is unwilling to commit himself to a single measure a number of approaches can be adopted:

(i)   The commonest - and often the default function - is a simple 0/1 loss function. All kinds of misclassification are treated as equally undesirable and all kinds of correct classification are treated as equally desirable.

(ii)   In presenting final performance results of a classification algorithm, there is no reason to restrict oneself to a single measure. One can pass the buck - in the form of a classification table - back to the researcher (physician, etc.).

(iii)   Aitchison et al (1977) suggested the use of "atypicality indices". These measure how closely a point x resembles the various classes by calculating the total probability (for a particular class) over regions in which the probability (density) is greater than the probability (density) at x. For example, if normal class conditional distributions are assumed then the atypicality indices are the integrals of the densities over the hypervolumes within hyperellipsoidal contours. For categorical data assessment of atypicality indices resulting from kernel estimates will be straightforward, but for continuous data it is more difficult.

(iv)   Other methods include the use of the reject option to force hesitation about uncertain decisions.

In designing the classifier (in the context of kernel classifiers the word "designing" means estimating the spread parameters, selecting the variables, and perhaps choosing a subset of the design sample - see Section 6.1) we have to choose a loss function. Assuming that we are not in an ideal situation - that the loss function has not been specified - what should we do?. The 0/1 loss function represents in some sense a <u>minimum information</u> loss function. Any other function assumes that some types of classification have more weight than others. The 0/1 loss function is also <u>symmetric</u>. Weighting misclassifications unequally will result in a poorer measure than weighting them equally if it subsequently turns out that the weighting should have gone in the opposite direction. The 0/1 loss function is thus in a sense minimax.

For these reasons the discussion in much of the rest of the chapter is formulated in terms of the 0/1 loss function. Most of the conclusions and warnings apply also to other functions.

Actually estimating the error rate (the 0/1 loss) of a classifier poses interesting theoretical and practical problems and important advances have been made only in the last ten years. We expand on this in the next section, where we outline the most advanced error rate estimation methods and explain the difficulties underlying the problem.

In Section 5.3 we briefly summarise some apparently counterintuitive phenomena which apply to the relationship between dimensionality, error rate, and design set size. The theoretical problems associated with choosing sets of variables are explained.

In Section 5.4 we consider alternative loss functions which can be used in place of the (computationally expensive) estimation of error rate for variable selection.

Finally, for completeness, a lightning survey is given in Section 5.5 of algorithms for actually choosing variables.

5.2   ERROR RATE ESTIMATION

Perhaps one's first thought on encountering the problem of how to estimate a classifier's error rate is that it is simple. One merely counts the number of design set points misclassified by the classifier and takes the ratio of this to the total number of design set points. This straightforward ("resubstitution") method has been proposed and used in the past. However, as a moment's thought shows, it has a serious drawback. Classifications are made by comparing the point, $\underline{x}$, to be classified, with the design set points $\{\underline{x}_1, \ldots, \underline{x}_N\}$. This is the case with all classifiers - whether based on nonparametric kernel estimates or on parameterised distributional assumptions (though the latter extract relevant information - the parameter estimates - from the design set). Thus one might expect the classifier to favour the design set points. Put another way, the classifier has been designed to optimise some function of the design set points (perhaps even the design set error rate itself) so it is hardly surprising that it performs better on this particular set of points than on other (future) points. In brief the estimate obtained by reclassifying the design set is over-optimistic.

170

Some examples of the optimistic nature of this estimate are given in Hand (1982a). This study, already referred to in Chapter 4, involved several different data sets, all with binary variables and all divided into independent design and test sets. Full details of the results are given in Hand (1982a) and here we merely summarise some of the relevant ones.

Data Set (1). This data came from a study of the effectiveness of a treatment for enuresis (Dische et al, 1982). There were 10 variables, two classes, and the design and test sets had respective sizes of 113 and 62. The classifier used a product kernel with the same λ in each dimension but different λ's for each class. Two methods for estimating the λ's were used: modified maximum likelihood (Section 4.3.2) and Hall's second order method (Section 4.3.3). The first column of Table 5.1 shows the results.

Data Set (2). This data arose during a study of how patterns of psychological distress in patients influence the type of psychotropic drugs prescribed. The design set had 167 points, the test set had 168, there were 5 variables and three classes. The classifiers were as in (1) and the results are shown in column two of Table 5.1.

Data Set (3). As data set (2) but using 12 variables.

TABLE 5.1

Optimistic nature of resubstitution estimate of error rate.
(a) Modified maximum likelihood estimate of λ.   (b) Hall estimate of
λ.   The table gives design and test set proportions misclassified.

(a)

	Enuresis	Psychodrug	Psychodrug	Mental Health
	(d = 10)	(d = 5)	(d = 12)	(d = 8)
Design Set	.177	.395	.144	.221
Test Set	.323	.435	.423	.393

(b)

	Enuresis	Psychodrug	Psychodrug	Mental Health
	(d = 10)	(d = 5)	(d = 12)	(d = 8)
Design Set	.177	.389	.144	.186
Test Set	.323	.435	.435	.393

172

Data Set (4). This data was collected during the development of a screening questionnaire to identify individuals likely to be suffering from psychiatric illness. The design and test sets each had 140 points, there were three classes, and 8 variables were studied. The results comprise column 4 of Table 5.1.

The optimistic nature of the resubstitution method is made strikingly obvious by the results in Table 5.1. In one case the design set error rate is only 26% of the test set error rate. (Another particularly noteworthy aspect of these results is the difference in design set error rate between columns 2 and 3. Presumably this is partly due to the greater sparseness of the observation points in the 12 dimensional space. This is discussed in Hand, 1982a).

An illustration of the optimism of the design set error rate for continuous variables is given in Figure 5.1. This data comes from Table 3 of Habbema and Hermans (1977). The top curve is the error rate estimated by the leaving-one-out method (see below). The bottom curve is that obtained by straightforward reclassification of the design set. Again the inadequacy of the latter estimate is made obvious - as is the fact that it becomes progressively poorer (more optimistic) as the number of variables increases.

Now that the danger of using the crude apparent error rate as an estimate of the true error rate has been illustrated we should at least remark that sometimes such a procedure may be acceptable. If the design set is large enough the optimistic bias introduced by the above will be very small. This is shown at the end of Section 2.3 where we quote Glick's (1972) result that the apparent error rate is a consistent estimator of the optimum rate.

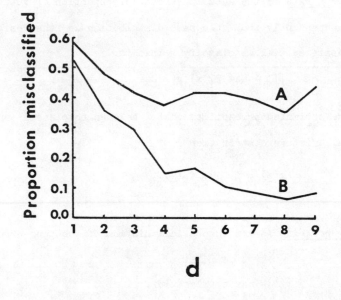

Figure 5.1 Leaving-one-out error estimate
(A) and resubstitution estimate (B) for the
first example in Habbema and Hermans (1977,
table 3).

174

Having noted that the problem of error rate estimation is more difficult than it might at first seem, we shall begin the discussion of alternative ways of tackling it by defining some terms.

(a)   The <u>apparent error rate</u> (or <u>resubstitution rate</u>) is the estimate discussed above - the proportion of design set points misclassified.

(b)   The <u>true error rate</u> is the actual asymptotic proportion of future samples (drawn independently from the same distribution as the design set) that the classifier will misclassify. That is,

$$\int \{1 - \max_i \hat{\pi}_i(\underline{x})\} g(\underline{x}) d\underline{x}$$

where $\hat{\pi}_i(\underline{x})$ is the estimated probability that $\underline{x}$ belongs to class i and $g(\underline{x})$ is the overall mixture distribution

$$g(\underline{x}) = \sum_{i=1}^{c} \pi_i \, f_i(\underline{x}).$$

(c)   The <u>Bayes error rate</u> is the theoretical minimum of the true error rate:

$$\int \{1 - \max_i \pi_i(\underline{x})\} g(\underline{x}) d\underline{x}.$$

where

$$\pi_i(\underline{x}) = f_i(\underline{x}) \pi_i / g(\underline{x}).$$

(d)   The <u>estimated true error rate</u> is an estimate of (b).

We would like to know the value of (b) but must content ourselves with (d). Immediately a whole area is opened up as we ask the obvious question - which estimator should we use?

This problem has been the focus of a considerable amount of research effort. Toussaint (1974) produced an extensive bibliography of work in the area. Other general discussions include Lachenbruch (1975, p.29 et seq), Fukunaga (1972, Section 5.4) and Hand (1981b, Section 8.1). The word "general" occurs in the preceding sentence because, as will be obvious from a perusal of these references, a considerable proportion of the work focusses on parametric classifiers (the most common being the assumption of multivariate normal class conditional distributions). Here, of course, we will concentrate on methods which do not require such assumptions - and which can be applied with the kernel method. We will, in fact, discuss two methods in detail, the cross validatory (or leaving-one-out) method and the bootstrap method. The cross validatory method can be approached from a number of different directions, and we shall begin with an informal approach before developing it from a more mathematical point of view.

The introductory discussion of the over-optimistic results of the apparent error rate make it clear that a possible approach would be to divide the available data into two sets. The classifier could be designed on one set and validated (i.e. its error rate estimated) on the other set. Obviously, however, such an approach is not ideal. The decision rule which results would not be the best we could obtain since it would be based on only part of the data. An improvement might be obtained if we subsequently re-defined the classifier, now basing it on the entire data set. Admittedly our error rate estimate would be only a rough approximation to the error rate of the final classifier, but that would be better than nothing.

This idea can easily be extended. Let us divide the entire data set into ten equal parts. Then, for each part in turn, classify the points in that part on the basis of the classifier designed on the other nine parts. The final estimate of error rate is then the average of the ten resulting estimates. The final classifier is found using the entire data set. That we might expect this to be an improvement on the method where we divide the data into two parts is easily seen. At each of the ten stages our error rate estimate is based on classifying an independent test set. Moreover each of the ten design sets comprises nine-tenths of the complete set and so will not be very different from it.

Now, of course, there is no reason why we should not extend this process to the limit. If N is the total design set size then we can consider each point in turn and classify it using the other (N-1) points. The proportion of the N points which are misclassified is the final error rate estimate. The final classifier is, of course, based on the entire set of N points - and differs from any one of the N classifiers used during the estimation in only a single point.

This is the leaving-one-out method. Now let us consider the more mathematical derivation.

In Sections 3.4 and 4.3.2 we introduced the method of cross validation and used it to estimate the smoothing parameters. The basic approach was to formulate some criterion function J(h), a function of a smoothing parameter, h, of the form

$$J(h) = \frac{1}{N} \sum_{i=1}^{N} L\{v_i, \hat{v}_i(h)\} \qquad (5.2.1)$$

where v_i was a function of the ith design set point and $\hat{v}_i(h)$ was a predicted value for v_i (the prediction being based on h and on the reduced set $\{\underline{x}_1,\ldots,\underline{x}_{i-1},\underline{x}_{i+1},\ldots,\underline{x}_N\}$), and where L was a suitable loss function. The estimate was then obtained by minimising the average loss J(h) by choice of h. The same approach can be used to estimate the performance of a classifier - and in particular it can be used to estimate the true error rate. To do this we let v_i be the known class of the ith design set point and $\hat{v}_i(h)$ be the predicted class based on the reduced design set with point $\underline{x}_i$ omitted. The loss function is simply

$$L(a,b) = \begin{matrix} 0 \text{ if } a=b \\ 1 \text{ if } a\neq b \end{matrix}$$

This is thus the same as the above informal leaving-one-out method.

In fact in this discussion we have glossed over the choice of h. Ideally the entire classifier should be defined afresh for each of the N points. For the kernel classifier this means that, in addition to specifying the (N-1) point design set each time, we should also recompute a value for h. This point is discussed immediately below.

It is obvious that one drawback of the cross validation or leaving-one-out method is the amount of computation involved. To estimate the error rate N distinct classifiers have to be designed. If some way can be devised to ease this computational burden then the method becomes much more attractive. For the case of classical discriminant analysis, Fukunaga and Kessell (1971) (see also Lachenbruch, 1975 (but beware of misprints in the published formulae); Fukunaga, 1972) present a way of easing this burden. They reformulate the problem so that the result of a classification based on a reduced design set is a simple modification of the classification based on the entire (N point) set. Thus the additional burden to recompute the classifications of the N points is minor once the complete set classifications are known. The question is, can we do the same for the kernel classifier?

If h is given a priori, and is not to be estimated from the data, then there is no problem. Each point $\underline{x}_i$ can easily be classified by the remaining (N-1) points - and less computation is involved than would be in calculating the apparent error rate (which is not to say it is a small amount of computation!). If h is to be estimated separately for each of the N sets of (N-1) points, however, then more work is involved. It seems not unreasonable to hope that the removal of a single point will not affect the estimate of h to a great extent (Fukunaga and Kessell (1971), on the choice of α in $h = n^{-\alpha/d}$, say "it does not appear that the choice of α is of critical importance", though the smallest sample they consider has 100 points. Scott and Factor (1981), in a study with $n = N = 26$ (one class), suggest that the position of an outlying point can substantially affect the result). One is tempted to suggest using a common h estimate in each of the N evaluations, the common estimate being obtained from the complete data set. Naturally such an approach is not justified in theory because of the biasing effect it will have on the result (the design sets now partly include all of the N points in the N cases), though it becomes less important as N increases.

The other major error rate estimation method, the bootstrap approach, is a more recent development. A description of the general method, plus examples in other estimation problems, is given in Efron (1979). The method has a striking simplicity and elegance, as will be made apparent if we begin the discussion by considering it in a general framework.

So, suppose that we wish to estimate a parameter $\theta(f)$, where we have used the argument f to make explicit the fact that θ depends on the underlying population distribution $f(x)$. Let $t(X)$ be an estimator of θ, based on the sample $X = \{x_1, \ldots, x_n\}$. Now if we can find an expression for the distribution of

$$R(X,f) = t(X) - \theta(f) \qquad (5.2.2)$$

we can estimate θ by

$$t(X) - E\{R(X,f)\} \qquad (5.2.3)$$

The elegance of the method arises from the clever way of estimating the distribution of $R(X,f)$. First define the distribution f^* by

$$f^*(x) = \begin{cases} \dfrac{1}{n} & \text{when } x \in X \\ 0 & \text{otherwise} \end{cases}$$

This can be regarded as an approximation to f. Thus, for any statement about f and its parameters we can make a matching statement about f^* and its parameters. And of course, the parameters of f^* are known since f^* is known. The same is not true of f. In particular, suppose that we draw, with replacement, a random sample of size n from X. Denote this by $X^* = \{x_1^*, \ldots, x_n^*\}$. Then $\theta(f^*)$ and $t(X^*)$ and so $R(X^*,f^*)$ can be calculated - and $R(X^*,f^*)$ is an approximation to $R(X,f)$. Thus, finally, we can estimate the distribution of $R(X,f)$ by the distribution of $R(X^*,f^*)$.

In general the distribution of $R(X^*,f^*)$ can be derived from theory, by Monte Carlo approximation, or by approximation via Taylor series expansions (which leads to the jackknife method). We shall adopt the

180

Monte Carlo method in our estimation of error rates.

Turning to the special case of error rate estimation, we shall concentrate on the two class case and on estimating the probability of misclassifying a point from just one of those classes (this permits straightforward generalisation to the multiclass case and also permits the comparison of different types of misclassification). The equivalent form to (5.2.2) is

$$R\{X_1,X_2),(f_1,f_2)\} = \text{(apparent error rate)} - \text{(true error rate)}$$

where $X_1 = \{x_{11},\ldots,x_{1n}\}$ is the design set for class 1, with population distribution $f_1(x)$, and where $X_2 = \{x_{21},\ldots,x_{2m}\}$ and $f_2(x)$ are for class 2. The final error rate estimate, equivalent to (5.2.3) is

$$\text{(apparent error rate)} - E\{R\{(X_1,X_2),(f_1,f_2)\}\}.$$

As in the general description, we substitute for f_1 and f_2 the approximations f_1^* and f_2^* where

$$f_1^*(x) = \begin{cases} \frac{1}{n} & \text{if } x \in X_1 \\ 0 & \text{otherwise} \end{cases} \qquad f_2^*(x) = \begin{cases} \frac{1}{m} & \text{if } x \in X_2 \\ 0 & \text{otherwise} \end{cases}$$

and we draw from f_1^* and f_2^* random samples X_1^* and X_2^* of size n and m (the size of X_1 and X_2) respectively. Now, let $\nu(A,B)$ be the number of points in a set A misclassified by the kernel classifier, based on set B. Concentrating on the first class, we have

$$R\{(X_1^*,X_2^*),(f_1^*,f_2^*)\} = \text{(estimate of apparent error rate)}$$
$$- \text{(estimate of true error rate)}.$$

$$= \frac{\nu(X_1^*,(X_1^*,X_2^*))}{n} - \frac{\nu(X_1,(X_1^*,X_2^*))}{n}$$

Repeating this for a number of samples X_1^* and X_2^* gives an estimate $\hat{E}$ of $E\{R\{X_1^*,X_2^*\}, (f_1^*,f_2^*)\}\}$. Thus, finally, the error rate estimate is

$$\frac{\nu(X_1,(X_1,X_2)}{n} - \hat{E}.$$

The question naturally arises as to which of these two methods, cross validation or bootstrap, is better. Efron (1979) shows an example of the bootstrap method outperforming the cross validation method, but this is with a simple linear discriminant function. This comparison seems a fruitful area for further research.

From a computational point of view neither method is quick. The bootstrap method requires generation of many random subsamples and estimation of smoothing parameters and classifications based on those parameters. As we have already noted, the cross validation method ideally requires n_i recalculations of the smoothing parameter(s) for class i. Again the search for a quicker (perhaps an approximate) way to achieve these error rate estimates might be fruitful. It should be noted, however, that for moderately large sample sizes there will usually be little difference between the two estimates. Indeed, if the design set is large enough the apparent error rate will be sufficiently close to the true error rate for most practical purposes.

While discussing error rate estimation we should note that if the reject option is being used (Chapter 6) then it is possible to estimate the error rate from a test set of unclassified samples.

There is one other point that needs to be made regarding the use to which these error rate estimates are put. If they are used to help in choosing between classifiers (or between h estimation methods or whatever) then a slightly paradoxical situation arises. This is most easily seen when we consider the use of an independent test set to give error estimates. Suppose we are to choose which classifier to use on the basis of the error rates on this test set. Then, in a sense, the test set is being used to design the classifier. The design set permits us (for example) to estimate the smoothing parameters and the test set permits us to choose one from a number of classifiers. But the role is similar. Just as the resubstitution method of error rate estimation is optimistic because the classifier has been designed to minimise design set misclassification (or some related function) so an underestimate will result if we use the test set results to choose a classifier and then take as our error estimate that test set rate. Clearly the problem will not be as grave as simply using the resubstitution method but it should still be avoided. The point is that a final estimate of error rate should not have been used during the classifier design or selection stages.

To illustrate some of the points discussed in this section compare Table 5.2 with Table 5.1. Table 5.2 contains leaving-one-out error estimates for the four data sets discussed above. (Using Aitchison and Aitken type product kernels. Unfortunately, at the time of writing, the bootstrap program has not been completed.) As expected, the leaving-one-out estimates are much larger than the apparent error rate values and are very close to the test set rates. A curious point worthy of note here is that the leaving-one-out estimates are all in fact slightly larger than the corresponding test set rates.

Table 5.3(a) gives the apparent misclassification rates for different (λ_1, λ_2) pairs using an Aitchison and Aitken product kernel on the enuresis data. Table 5.3(b) gives corresponding leaving-one-out estimates. In Chapter 4 we presented the test set results for this

TABLE 5.2

Leaving-one-out error estimates for the same data as used in Table 5.1.
(a) Modified maximum likelihood λ estimation   (b) Hall λ estimation.

(a)

Enuresis	Psychodrug	Psychodrug	Mental Health
(d = 10)	(d = 5)	(d = 12)	(d = 8)
.363	.533	.503	.400

(b)

Enuresis	Psychodrug	Psychodrug	Mental Health
(d = 10)	(d = 5)	(d = 12)	(d = 8)
.327	.557	.515	.400

TABLE 5.3

(a) Apparent error rates for Aitchison and Aitken product kernel on enuresis data at different values of λ_1 and λ_2.   (b) The corresponding leaving-one-out estimates.

(a)

λ_1

		.6	.7	.8	.9
	.6	.292	.469	.460	.442
	.7	.407	.230	.354	.407
λ_2	.8	.407	.310	.177	.230
	.9	.389	.327	.204	.177

(b)

λ_1

		.6	.7	.8	.9
	.6	.389	.504	.487	.496
	.7	.451	.345	.478	.504
λ_2	.8	.434	.469	.327	.442
	.9	.460	.425	.372	.354

situation. The interesting thing here is that in each row and each column the smallest error rates occur when $\lambda_1 = \lambda_2$. This is true for both apparent error rate and leaving-one-out rate (and test set error rate). If one were to choose a (λ_1, λ_2) pair from those shown here, on the basis of the leaving-one-out rate, this would lead to the pair which minimised the test set error rate. We are certainly not suggesting that either of these properties is universal, but are merely pointing them out as of interest and worth further investigation.

Any purported universality of the first property is destroyed by the results of the similar analysis of the mental health data (classes 1 and 2 only) shown in Table 5.4. Once again, however, choosing the (λ_1, λ_2) pair to be that which minimises the leaving-one-out rate leads to one of the several pairs which minimise the test set error rate (see Chapter 4, Table 4.5 for the matching table of test set rates).

5.3   ON CHOOSING VARIABLES

In any kind of multivariate statistical analysis it is necessary to make decisions about which variables to study. Often the decision whether or not to include a particular variable is clear. In a study of scholastic achievement, for example, a measure of the number of pets owned by housekeepers in the town in which the subject was born would probably be irrelevant. On the other hand, measures of the staff-to-pupil ratio during the subject's school education would certainly be worth considering. Sometimes, however, the decision is not so clear. Indeed it is usually the case that one can think of dozens or even hundreds of variables which might influence the result

TABLE 5.4

(a) Apparent error rates for Aitchison and Aitken product kernel on classes 1 and 2 of the mental health data at different values of λ_1 and λ_2. (b) The corresponding leaving-one-out estimates.

(a)

λ_1

		.92	.94	.96	.98
	.92	.168	.168	.147	.126
	.94	.168	.147	.147	.126
λ_2	.96	.147	.147	.147	.126
	.98	.147	.147	.147	.126

(b)

λ_1

		.92	.94	.96	.98
	.92	.326	.305	.295	.211
	.94	.337	.316	.305	.242
λ_2	.96	.326	.337	.316	.263
	.98	.326	.337	.347	.274

(in our case the "result" is the classification of the object). Moreover it might be the case that transformed variables will be more relevant than untransformed variables. For example, height cubed (being linearly related to volume and mass) might be a better variable to use in a study of slimming diet than height itself. Should one then simply include all possible variables and their transformations that one can think of? In this section we consider this question.

An immediate - and negative - answer to the above question is prompted by the simple fact of cost. On the one hand we have the computational burden associated with very large numbers of variables, and on the other hand we have the expense of collecting the data in the first place. But, one would be unwilling to risk sacrificing crucial information by not measuring possibly relevant variables. The answer is thus to measure as large a number of variables as is practically feasible <u>for the design set</u> and then analyse these to select a highly effective subset of variables. New points to be classified are measured only on this subset. This is exactly analogous to the use of pilot surveys to design a small and effective questionnaire (e.g. Goldberg, 1972).

Cost, of whatever kind, is an obvious motive for wishing to reduce the number of variables used. There is, however, another reason, and one which is altogether more subtle. This reason leads, as well as to dimensionality reduction by selection of variables, to dimensionality reduction by transformation.

This second reason is a superficially rather bizarre relationship between error rate and dimensionality. For a given design set it is found that the error rate initially decreases and then begins to increase as d increases. One might have expected, since each additional variable can only add information and not remove it, that the error rate would decrease monotonically (and certainly not increase) with increasing d. Explanations for the U-shaped error/d curve hinge around (i) the poorer representativeness of a fixed size of design sample as d increases and (ii) the increased flexibility of the decision surface as d increases (so that it follows the data more closely). An extensive discussion is given in Hand (1981b). We will not go into further details here, but will simply give some examples.

First we take an extreme case. We consider a situation in which the additional variables are known to contribute no information at all. This means that adding them is unlikely to improve the performance of the classifier (though it can do so) but is quite likely to degrade it. (Under less extreme conditions the question of whether or not to include a variable is answered by asking whether or not the additional information it provides outweighs the degradation caused by including it). We will illustrate this extreme situation with four data sets.

The first consists of data generated from two standard multivariate normal classes separated on one and only one variable. The prior probabilities are 0.2 and 0.8. In this situation, of course, the optimum decision surface is a hyperplane perpendicular to the variable on which the two classes differ. If that variable alone was used in the kernel analysis then the resulting decision surface would be such a hyperplane (though probably not in exactly the optimal position) - or, possibly, a set of such hyperplanes. However, when many additional variables are also used the decision surface in the kernel method becomes markedly non-linear - it deviates from the optimal form.

Figure 5.2(a) illustrates plots of error rate against dimensionality for samples of size 10, 25, and 50 and for separations of 1.0 and 2.0 between the classes.

The second data set is as the first but has class prior probabilities of 0.5. Figure 5.2(b) shows the results.

Figures 5.3(a) and (b) show similar plots for the third and fourth data sets: multivariate lognormal distributions with priors (a) 0.2 and 0.8, (b) 0.5 and 0.5.

In all four of the above studies product kernels with normal factors with h = 1.1 were used.

Similar graphs can be derived from Van Ness and Simpson (1976) and Van Ness (1979) - and the latter hint at something more complex. The data comes from two normal classes with equal priors and respective covariance matrices

$$\underline{\Sigma}_1 = \underline{I} \qquad \underline{\Sigma}_2 = \underline{I}/2$$

Figure 5.4 shows the case when h is forced to be the same in each class while Figure 5.5 shows the situation when different h's are allowed for the two classes. (Van Ness's method for choosing h's is described in Chapter 3. It sets $h_2 = \alpha h_1$ where α is proportional to the ratio of the average of the roots of the diagonals of the sample covariance matrix of class 2 to the corresponding average for class 1). As can be seen, permitting different h's in the two classes can lead to an improvement in misclassification rate as d increases. It would be interesting to investigate this further.

An example on real data is given in Habbema and Hermons (1977, Table 3). We have extracted the relevant results and plotted them in Figure 5.1. Curve A is the error rate estimated by the leaving-one-out

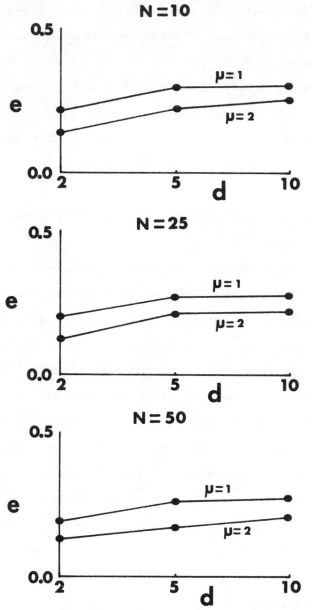

Figure 5.2(a) Misclassification rates (e) for
data from two standard multivariate normal
classes separated a distance μ on only one variable.
Product kernels with normal factors and h=1.1
were used. The class priors were 0.2 and 0.8.

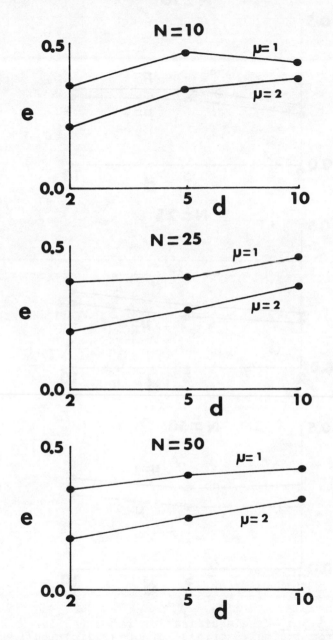

<u>Figure 5.2(b)</u> As Figure 5.2(a) but with priors
0.5 and 0.5.

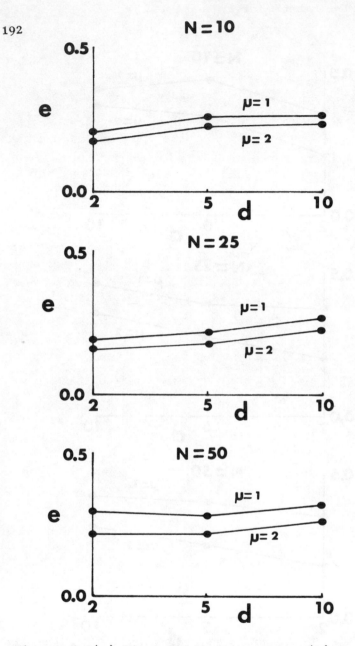

Figure 5.3(a) Misclassification rates (e) for
data from two multivariate lognormal distributions,
identical except that one has been shifted a
distance μ on one variable. Product kernels with
normal factors and h=1.1 were used. The class
priors were 0.2 and 0.8.

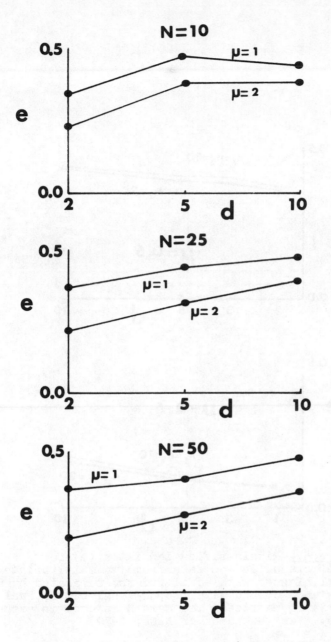

Figure 5.3(b) As Figure 5.3(a) but with priors 0.5 and 0.5.

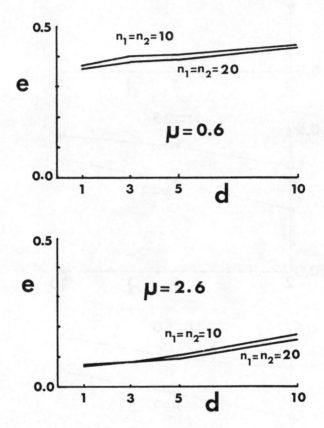

<u>Figure 5.4</u> Misclassification rates (e) for
kernel classifier on data from two multivariate
normal classes with equal priors, separated by
a distance μ, and with proportional but unequal
covariance matrices. The same h is used in each
class. (See text and Van Ness, 1979).

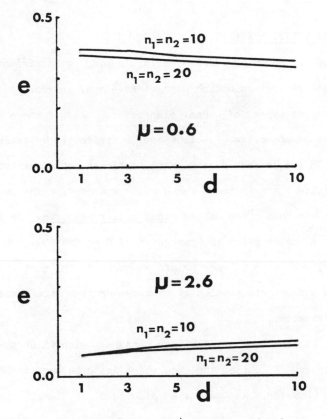

Figure 5.5 As Figure 5.4 but permitting different h's for each class (see text and Van Ness, 1979).

method. Note that it is clear from this that the error/dimensionality relationship need not be smooth (and also that the peculiarities of real data mean that there might be more than one local minimum). The initial improvement as d increases is apparent.

5.4   SEPARABILITY MEASURES

The problem of choosing variables is in many ways similar to the problem of estimating smoothing parameters - and, indeed, to choosing between different types of kernel classifier. All of these problems begin with some objective function and optimise it by estimation or selection. In the present case we wish to find a set of variables for which the classes are in some sense well separated. The criteria in this context are thus often called separability measures. An extensive general discussion is given in Chapter 6 of Hand (1981b), but here we content ourselves with a very brief summary of the most widely used measures and a short description of measures derived from ideas related to kernel estimates.

The best criterion - or separability measure - with which to compare variable sets is, of course, the one which is to be used in the final classifier. However, as we have discussed at length in earlier chapters, it will usually not be possible to use this ideal criterion. Moreover, as we commented earlier in this chapter, computational costs often mean that some criterion simpler than the ideal one must be adopted.

First, let us consider what is perhaps the most obvious initial choice: error rate. It is clear that apparent error rate is not good enough and that some better estimate, such as those discussed in Section 5.2, must be used. It is also clear from Section 5.2 that these estimates may be excluded from the bounds of possibility by their time requirements. In choosing a subset of variables one would ideally wish to compare all subsets of size i from D for i = 1,...,d' (where D is the original total number of variables and d' is the maximum size of subset one wishes to consider). This means that there are

$$M = \sum_{i=1}^{d'} \binom{D}{i}$$

subsets of variables to compare. This can easily be a very large number.

On the other hand, one must remember that selection of variables is a process that need only be carried out once. It is probably worthwhile expending a fair proportion of the resources during the design stage to ensure more accurate classifications later. Habbema and Hermans (1977) argue in favour of using estimated error rate as the selection criterion. Moreover in Section 5.5 we discuss ways to accelerate the search through the M subsets.

We now mention a few of the measures other than error rate which have been used. One of the most popular separability measures is Wilks's lambda, the ratio of the determinants of the within class to total data scatter matrices. This is equivalent to the usual multivariate F statistic used in testing equality of the group mean vectors. This criterion and those equivalent to it have the disadvantage that in

multiple class situations they do not concentrate on the least
separable classes (which will contribute relatively large amounts to
the misclassification rate - subject to any qualification due to
unequal class sizes, of course). Other criteria which do do this can
easily be devised by applying any separability measure to the two
closest classes. Thus one could apply Wilks's lambda to the two
closest groups. Other criteria (such as MINRESID in Nie et al, 1975,
p.447) combine separability measures from all pairs of groups. Rao's V
is another common way of combining between group separability measures
to form a global multiclass measure.

Several measures have been considered which have a known relationship
with error rate for certain kinds of distribution (the F-ratio is, of
course, one of these). Others are the divergence (Kullback, 1968), the
Chernoff distance, and the Bhattacharyya distance. The latter two
measures provide bounds on the error rate. Unfortunately, if the
distributions are not known to be of the forms permitting
simplification then multivariate integration - or a Monte Carlo
estimation - is required. In such a case one might as well use error
rate itself as the separability measure. Detailed discussion of
separability measures is contained in Hand (1981b) and Kittler (1975).

Although the separability measures introduced above have been used
with categorical variables, most of them are designed for continuous
variables. Measures specifically aimed at categorical data include the
average logarithmic score and the average quadratic score. Both of
these are based on the notion that ideally the estimated probability of
belonging to class i should be large for points which do come from
class i. Thus the larger is

$$J = \frac{1}{N} \sum_{i=1}^{N} \log \hat{\pi}(\underline{y}_i \mid \underline{x}_1, \ldots, \underline{x}_N)$$

(where $\hat{\pi}(\underline{y}_i \mid \underline{x}_1, \ldots, \underline{x}_N)$ is the estimated posterior probability of the class that $\underline{y}_i$ is known to belong to) the better is the separation between the classes. $\{\underline{y}_i\}$ could be a test set or $\hat{\pi}$ could be evaluated by the leaving-one-out method - so $\underline{y}_i \in \{\underline{x}_1, \ldots, \underline{x}_N\}$, the design set. Similarly, the average quadratic score

$$J = \frac{1}{N} \sum_{i=1}^{N} \{(1 - \hat{\pi}_1(\underline{y}_i \mid \underline{x}_1, \ldots, \underline{x}_N))^2 +$$

$$\sum_{j=2}^{c} \hat{\pi}_j (\underline{y}_i \mid \underline{x}_1, \ldots, \underline{x}_N)^2\}$$

($\hat{\pi}_j(\underline{y}_i \mid \underline{x}_1, \ldots, \underline{x}_N)$ being the posterior probability estimate for class j at point $\underline{y}_i$) is larger the better is the separation.

None of the measures so far described have any special relationship with the kernel method. A few measures which do have such a relationship have been developed but in general one should remember that the crude kernel method is not a quick classifier. It involves a large data set - and hence a lot of computation - and separability measures based on it will not satisfy the desirable separability measure property of permitting quick evaluation.

Nevertheless Koontz and Fukunaga (1972) describe the criterion

$$J = \sum_{j<i}^{N} \sum^{N} K(x_i, x_j) \, I(x_i, x_j)$$

where K is the kernel function and I is an index function given by

$$I(a,b) = \begin{array}{l} 1 \text{ if } a \neq b \\ 0 \text{ if } a=b \end{array}$$

Although they do not recommend its use in variable selection the authors do point out that it could be used in this way.

Patrick and Fischer (1969) present a measure for the two class case which makes even more direct use of kernel estimators:

$$J = \{\int\{\frac{\pi_1}{n_1} \sum_{j=1}^{n_1} \frac{1}{h_1^d} K(\frac{x - x_j^{(1)}}{h_1})$$

$$- \frac{\pi_2}{n_2} \sum_{j=1}^{n_2} \frac{1}{h_2^d} K(\frac{x - x_j^{(2)}}{h_2})\}^2 \, dx\}^{\frac{1}{2}}$$

where $x_j^{(i)}$ is the jth design set element of class i. They show that if $h_1 = h_2$ (not, the reader will recall from earlier discussions, a desirable constraint to impose) and if one is using normal kernels:

$$J = \{\sum_{j=1}^{n_1} \sum_{k=1}^{n_1} \phi_{jk}^{11} + \sum_{j=1}^{n_2} \sum_{k=1}^{n_2} \phi_{jk}^{22} - 2\sum_{j=1}^{n_1} \sum_{k=1}^{n_2} \phi_{jk}^{12}\}^{\frac{1}{2}} \qquad (5.4.1)$$

with

$$\phi_{jk}^{rs} = \frac{\pi_r \pi_s}{n_r n_s} \{\frac{1}{h\sqrt{2\pi}}\}^d \exp\{-\frac{1}{4h^2}||x_j^r - x_k^s||^2\}$$

We shall return to this criterion below.

5.5   SELECTION ALGORITHMS

In Section 5.3 we explained the reasons for reducing the number of variables. These included the cost of taking a large number of measurements (where "cost" is used in its technical statistical sense and might be in practical rather than financial terms) and the degradation in performance associated with having too many variables. One could use error rate (or a more general estimated loss) to compare sets of variables, or if this is impracticable one could use a simpler and quicker separability criterion such as those mentioned in Section 5.4. Even in the latter case, however, there may be too many subsets of variables to permit exhaustive search, so in this section we study accelerated ways of finding variables' subsets.

It is convenient (and traditional) to divide these ways into two groups. In the first group we restrict ourselves to studying subsets of the variables originally measured. In the second group we consider using a small number of functions of the original variables. The first type of approach would apply, for example, if it was expensive to continue taking all the original measurements on the objects to be classified and one wanted to take only a small subset. This sort of situation occurs frequently in sociological and psychological studies where the variables are questions in a questionnaire (and cost here is in subject's time rather than money). The second type of approach can be applied if our reason for eliminating variables is not cost of measurement but is, for example, the desire to eliminate redundancy in our classifier. Principal components analysis is an example of this second class of method.

Choosing a subset from the original set is clearly a combinatorial problem. There are $(2^D - 1)$ non-null subsets which can be chosen from D variables. If D is large - it is often 100 or more - then exhaustive search through these subsets is out of the question. We shall briefly discuss practical ways of tackling this problem.

We begin by thinking of the set of possible subsets as a space through which we wish to search to find that point which maximises an objective function. The objective function is our separability measure. Each point of the space corresponds to a subset of the set of D variables - and the points are related in terms of the mutual content of the corresponding subsets. Thus the space has a structure which we can utilise in devising accelerated search algorithms.

One particular class of accelerated search algorithm is especially popular. It also has the merit - not true of another algorithm we outline below - that its members can be applied with any separability criterion. In particular they can be applied with estimated error rate itself. This is the class of stepwise search algorithms. These algorithms make use of the ordered nature of the subset space. Thus a subset of size d can be built up sequentially, starting with one variable, adding another, and so on until there are d in all. Equally, we could start with the complete set and sequentially eliminate variables. The variable to add (eliminate) next is chosen on the basis that it leads to the maximum increase (smallest decrease) in the separation of the groups.

Obvious extensions of these methods include adding or eliminating groups of variables at a time, and alternately adding and eliminating variables. (For example, at each step add the set of three variables which leads to greatest improvement and eliminate the subset of two which detracts least from the performance.) Such methods are discussed in Hand (1981b).

A disadvantage of stepwise methods is that they merely find a local optimum, with no guarantee that it is global. The more complex methods (adding and eliminating groups of variables) are, of course, more likely to find the global optimum than the simpler ones but this is at an increased cost in computer time.

An alternative search method, which guarantees finding the global optimum, is the branch and bound algorithm. Unfortunately the branch and bound strategy avoids exhaustive search by making an assumption about the separability measure. If the assumption is not satisfied the algorithm should not be used. Let X, Y, and Z be arbitrary subsets of variables such that X is contained in Y and Y is contained in Z. Then the branch and bound method requires that the separation should change monotonically as we proceed from X to Z. For example, if J(W) is the value of the separability measure evaluated on subset W then

$$J(X) \leq J(Y) \leq J(Z)$$

for all subsets X, Y, Z such that X is in Y is in Z. the direction of the monotonic relationship can be inverted, provided it is still consistent. In the following explanation we shall assume that J increases with increasing size of subset.

It is obvious that with J increasing in this way our selection process will end up with the entire set of variables (this being the set which maximises J, the separability). This means that we shall have to modify our aim slightly and try to find that subset of a given size (d) which maximises J.

204

Suppose, then, that we start with the entire set and eliminate variables in our search for the d best. Suppose also that, during the course of our search, we have already found a subset V of d variables with criterion value J(V) greater than the criterion value of the subset of d'(>d) variables we are currently considering. Then there is no point in looking at the $\binom{d'}{d}$ sub-subsets of these d' variables. J can only decrease as we move from d' to d and we already have a subset (V) with a greater J value. This is the principle of the branch and bound search method. Further details are given in Hand (1981, 1981b).

Clearly estimated error rate is not a suitable criterion to use with the branch and bound method because it does not change monotonically with increasing d - unless one can be confident that one's desired number of variables does not involve a search which passes the lowest point of the error/dimensionality curve. (And this also assumes a regularly shaped curve. The irregularity of Figure 5.1 curve A suggests this is a risky assumption.)

We turn now to methods which find a small number of variables by transformation of the original large set. Once again, in principle, any criterion can be used. One simply decides what kind of transformation one wishes to apply (e.g. linear or not) and then estimates its parameters by an appropriate method of mathematical optimisation. The most widely used method is classical discriminant analysis. This finds the (C-1) dimensional subspace which maximises the between to within class dispersion. Details are given in any book on discriminant analysis, such as Lachenbruch (1975), or again in Hand (1981b). Classical discriminant analysis is a linear transformation - the axes defining the subspace are linear functions of the original variables. More generally, higher order terms can be used in the "linear" function - as is done in quadratic discrimination, for example. Once the subspace has been identified, of course, one abandons the linear or quadratic decision surface and uses a formal kernel method.

Neither the separability measures nor the transformation method here make direct use of kernel ideas, however. As we commented in the previous section, one reason for this is that measures related to the kernel idea do not permit speedy evaluation. Nevertheless Patrick and Fischer (1969) have applied their separability criterion in this situation. Once again they consider linear transformations. So, let A be a projection transformation projecting from the D dimensional space to the d dimensional subspace. Then

$$J(A) = \{\int\{\{\frac{\pi_1}{n_1}\sum_{j=1}^{n_1}\frac{1}{h_1^d}K\{A\{\frac{x - x_j^{(1)}}{h_1}\}\}$$

$$-\frac{\pi_2}{n_2}\sum_{j=1}^{n_2}\frac{1}{h_2^d}K\{A\{\frac{x - x_j^{(2)}}{h_2}\}\}\}^2 \ d\underline{x}\}^{\frac{1}{2}}$$

When $h_1 = h_2 = h$ and using normal kernels Patrick and Fischer show this reduces to (5.4.1) with

$$\phi_{jk}^{rs} = \frac{\pi_r \ \pi_s}{n_r \ n_s}\{\frac{1}{h\sqrt{2\pi}}\}^d \ \exp\{-\frac{1}{4h^2}||A(\underline{x}_j^{(r)} - \underline{x}_k^{(s)})||^2\}.$$

If h is large J can be shown to be a function of the interclass minus the intraclass Euclidean distances.

To maximise J with respect to A, Patrick and Fischer use the method of steepest descent, showing that the gradient of J, ∇J, can be expressed as

$$\nabla J(A) = \frac{-1}{4h^2 J(A)(2h\sqrt{\pi})^d} \times$$

$$\sum_{r=1}^{2} \sum_{s=1}^{2} \sum_{j=1}^{n_1} \sum_{k=1}^{n_2} \{\xi_{rs}\{\exp\{-\frac{1}{4h^2}||A(\underline{x}_j^{(r)} - \underline{x}_k^{(s)})||^2\}\}\} \Lambda_{jk}^{rs}$$

where Λ_{jk}^{rs} is the matrix with elements

$$(\lambda_{jk}^{rs})_{pq} = \{\underline{v}_p'(\underline{x}_j^{(r)} - \underline{x}_k^{(s)})\}(x_j^{(r)} - x_{kq}^{(s)})$$

(the subscript q on x referring to the qth component of the vector) and where $\underline{v}_p$ is a basis vector of the d dimensional subspace.

In fact, to ensure that A remains a projection map we must increment A in the direction of the component of $\nabla J(A)$ given by

$$\underline{\hat{w}}_i = \underline{w}_i - \sum_{j=1}^{d} (\underline{w}_i' \ \underline{v}_j)\underline{v}_j \quad 1 <= i < d.$$

where $\underline{w}_i$ is the ith row vector of $\nabla J(A)$.

Patrick and Fischer point out that this is a slow algorithm and suggest ways in which it might be accelerated. It almost goes without saying that kernel methods are ideally suited to parallel computer architectures.

CHAPTER 6
Other Topics

6.1   PREPROCESSING THE DESIGN SET

A property of the kernel method, as described in the body of this book, is that it requires the storage of a potentially large design set. This can be a disadvantage, as compared, for example, with adaptive parametric methods which need only a (relatively) few coefficients to be stored. Not only this, but it is clear from a comparison of the basic forms of the kernel classifier and simple parametric classifiers (such as Fisher's linear discriminant method) that the latter will produce quicker classifications. Sometimes speed of classification is an important factor in the choice between methods, and accuracy can be sacrificed (examples of situations where very large numbers of objects must be classified very quickly are the analysis of bubble chamber photographs and satellite pictures). Although recent advances in microelectronic technology (computer memory becoming cheaper; the development of parallel machines) mean that these disadvantages are becoming less serious we should at least consider how they might be faced - after all, not all users of the methods described here will have access to the latest hardware! (The reader should be aware that in fact the properties described here as disadvantages will usually cause no problems. Few situations have exorbitantly large data sets or require excessively quick calculations).

Several methods of preprocessing the design set to alleviate these problems for nearest neighbour classifiers have been developed (see Hand, 1981b, Chapter 2 for an extensive discussion). Unfortunately some of the methods might cause difficulty if applied directly to kernel methods. For example, the condensed nearest neighbour method (Hart, 1968) discards points far from regions of contention (e.g. far from the decision surface) and the edited nearest neighbour rule (Hand and Batchelor, 1978) discards points to smooth out the decision surface. In both cases discarding points might distort the resulting kernel probability estimates. The author knows of no published work applying such methods to, or modifying such methods for, kernel classifiers. On the other hand, the branch and bound method for identifying nearest neighbours developed by Fukunaga and Narendra (1975) could be applied to kernel classifiers using kernels of finite support. This method accelerates the classification process while using the entire design set.

An alternative approach has been suggested by Specht (1967a). This method approximates the kernel estimate by a polynomial function. In the two class case the decision surface formed by comparing the two kernel estimates is approximated by a polynomial. The method is elegant in that the apparent risk of overfitting the data is avoided - the data, per se, are not fitted by the polynomial decision surface, but rather the already smoothed kernel decision surface is fitted. Thus one can include as many terms in the series as one likes.

Very large numbers of design set elements can be handled by the method, as they are (adaptively) processed to yield improved estimates of the polynomial coefficients. It might seem that large numbers of terms would be needed in the polynomial expansion in order to obtain adequate accuracy - especially with large numbers of variables. Specht (1967), however, reports a study with 46 variables which shows very good results with only 30 terms. (But note that it is obvious from the nature of the data that the original 46 variables will be highly correlated.) It would be interesting to see how practical this extension of the kernel method is on other problems.

6.2   THE REJECT OPTION

The reject option is a concept which is not especially related to the kernel method but which is of sufficient importance that it should at least be mentioned in any book on discriminant analysis or pattern recognition. In many real situations an immediate classification is not vital and objects for which one cannot make a sufficiently confident classification can be (perhaps temporarily) put aside (Quesenberry and Gessaman, 1968; Habbema, Hermans, and van der Burght, 1974). In some medical diagnostic problems, for example, a patient could be referred for further tests. More tests could be carried out until a threshold of certainty had been reached. This (temporary) discarding is termed "rejection" - as opposed to "acceptance" for a classification.

Use of the reject option has several important implications. For example, it is true to say that a classifier with as small an error rate as one wishes can be achieved (ultimately one rejects all objects - and achieves a zero misclassification rate). Moreover, when the reject option is being used it is possible to estimate a classifier's error rate without knowledge of the classification of the test set points (see, for example, Fukunaga, 1972; Hand, 1981b). This can be useful if the original method of classification is expensive or impractical.

6.3   MIXED VARIABLE TYPES

The difficulty of handling problems where the variables are measured on different types of scales is a persistent and troublesome one in multivariate statistics. However, for discriminant analysis the use of the kernel method with product kernels renders the problem trivial, providing a direct and intuitively appealing solution. Suppose for example that there are d_1 interval scale variables $x_1, \ldots, x_{d_1}$, and $d_2 (= d - d_1)$ nominal scale variables $x_{d_1+1}, \ldots, x_d$. Then the overall kernel is

$$K(\underline{y}, \underline{x}) = \prod_{i=1}^{d_1} K_1(y_i, x_i) \prod_{i=d_1+1}^{d} K_2(y_i, x_i)$$

where K_1 is an interval scale univariate kernel and K_2 is the nominal scale kernel. Note, however, that there is concealed in this solution an implicit decision about the relative importance of the different types of variables. This decision can, of course, be made explicit - it is reflected in the sizes of the smoothing parameters.

Product kernels are the most widely applied type of kernel. The assumption of independence of variables _within_ the kernel does not imply a corresponding independence assumption for the overall class-conditional distributions.

6.4   MISSING DATA

The problem of missing data is a ubiquitous one in statistics, especially in multivariate statistics. The symmetry of analyses designed for complete descriptor vectors is lost when one tries to apply them to data sets containing incomplete vectors. This can mean that methods developed for such data are complicated and inelegant. For these reasons one of the most common approaches to handling such data is to discard any incomplete vectors. Sometimes such a Procrustean solution may be acceptable, but all too often it leads to an unacceptably large proportion of the data being excluded from the analysis. In any case, discarding a vector of 100 measurements merely because one is absent seems a tremendous waste of what information there is in the 99 observed scores. Moreover, if an object to be classified (for example, a patient to be diagnosed) has a missing value (he was unconscious on arrival at the hospital so they could not ask his age) discarding is hardly an acceptable solution.

For kernel methods the question of how to deal with incomplete descriptor vectors can be usefully divided into three parts - which are most conveniently asked in the reverse order from that one would need to answer in practice. First, how do we handle incomplete test vectors, assuming the probability estimates for the classes can be made? Second, how do we deal with incomplete design vectors, given values for the smoothing parameter? And third, how do we estimate smoothing parameters from incomplete design vectors?

One class of solutions which has been suggested for the first question can also be used for the other questions - and, indeed, for any multivariate statistical problem with incomplete data. This is to estimate substitute values for the missing items. A common method is to use the mean values of the corresponding components in the design set. Another method is to use an iterative series of regressions to predict missing values. These are simply attempts to complete the data set so that a standard analysis can be performed - but they risk biasing the result by inventing "data". An interesting and particularly simple method which can be seen as a replacement method for incomplete design vectors has been described by Titterington (1977) and we shall return to this below. For incomplete test points, however, the optimal method is quite straightforward to describe and use. It is simply to make classifications in the subspace of those components which are present. Thus, if components $y_{r+1}, \ldots, y_d$ are missing from a point $\underline{y}$ to be classified, the kernel estimate becomes

$$f(y) = \frac{1}{n} \sum_{i=1}^{n} \prod_{j=1}^{r} K(y_j, x_{ij})$$

If $\int K(u)du = 1$ then this is seen to be equivalent to integrating the d dimensional estimate over the missing variables (summing in the discrete case).

Incomplete design set vectors pose a more difficult problem. Titterington (1977) has examined a number of methods for binary variables and the extension to more general categorical variables seems straightforward. One method, referred to above, is particularly elegant. It is an extension of the Aitchison and Aitken (1976) kernel described in Chapter 4. This product kernel for binary variables, with different smoothing parameters in each dimension, is

$$K(\underline{x},\underline{y}) = \prod_{j=1}^{d} \lambda_j^{1-|x_j-y_j|} (1 - \lambda_j)^{|x_j-y_j|}$$

Titterington suggests setting

$$\lambda_j = \begin{cases} \frac{1}{2} & \text{if } y_j \text{ is missing} \\ \lambda_j & \text{if } y_j \text{ is observed} \end{cases} \qquad (6.4.1)$$

$\underline{y}$, here, is the design set vector.

Another of the methods investigated by Titterington (1977) is to treat "missing" as an extra category. We gave an example of a kernel using this approach in Section 4.2.

The third of the questions asked above, that of how to estimate the smoothing parameters, must depend on the estimation method one wishes to adopt. Using the method of Aitchison and Aitken (1976) and Titterington's suggestion in (6.4.1) estimation with binary variables is straightforward. Previously we found the smoothing parameer λ which maximised

$$J(\lambda) = \prod_{j=1}^{n} \sum_{\substack{i=1 \\ i \neq j}}^{n} \prod_{k=1}^{d} K(x_{kj}, x_{ki} \; ; \; \lambda)$$

where x_{kj} is the kth component of the jth design vector in this class. Now we maximise

$$J(\lambda) = \prod_{j=1}^{n} \sum_{\substack{i=1 \\ i \neq j}}^{n} \prod_{k=1}^{d} K_k(x_{kj}, x_{ki} \; ; \; \lambda)$$

with

$$K_k(x_{kj}, x_{ki}; \lambda) = \begin{cases} 1 \text{ if } x_{kj} \text{ ("test point") is missing} \\ K(x_{kj}, x_{ki}; \tfrac{1}{2}) \text{ if } x_{ki} \text{ ("design point") is missing} \\ K(x_{kj}, x_{ki}; \lambda) \text{ otherwise} \end{cases}$$

(If both x_{kj} and x_{ki} are missing then $K(x_{kj}, x_{kj}; \lambda) = 1$).

This can be extended to more general categorical variables quite easily, but the continuous variable case is more difficult - the difficulty arising because of incomplete design set vectors. The present author knows of no work on the use of kernel methods with incomplete continuous variable design vectors. It seems, however, that the idea of treating "missing" as a separate category might be a fruitful one for future research.

CHAPTER 7
Kernel Methods Versus The Rest

7.1 CONTINUOUS VARIABLES

In this chapter we summarise some of the published comparisons between kernel and other methods of discriminant analysis. The emphasis in this literature has been on continuous rather than categorical variables (reflecting the general trend in pattern recognition research) but recently, particularly from statistical sources, more attention has been paid to the special problems of categorical variables. This is to be commended in view of the importance of discrete variables in areas such as medicine and the behavioural sciences. As will be seen below, the most popular type of continuous variable comparison has been on synthetic data generated from normal distributions.

Gessaman and Gessaman (1972) performed a Monte-Carlo comparison on three two-class problems with bivariate normal distributions as follows:

(i) $\underline{\mu}_1 = (0,0)$, $\underline{\Sigma}_1 = \{\begin{smallmatrix} 1 & 0 \\ 0 & 1 \end{smallmatrix}\}$, $\underline{\mu}_2 = (2,0)$, $\underline{\Sigma}_2 = \{\begin{smallmatrix} 1 & 2 \\ 2 & 9 \end{smallmatrix}\}$

216

(ii) $\underline{\mu}_1 = (0,0), \underline{\Sigma}_1 = \{\begin{smallmatrix} 1 & 1 \\ 1 & 4 \end{smallmatrix}\}, \underline{\mu}_2 = (0,0), \underline{\Sigma}_2 = \{\begin{smallmatrix} 1 & -1 \\ -1 & 4 \end{smallmatrix}\}$

(iii) $\underline{\mu}_1 = (1,1), \underline{\Sigma}_1 = \{\begin{smallmatrix} 1 & 1 \\ 1 & 4 \end{smallmatrix}\}, \underline{\mu}_2 = (-1,0), \underline{\Sigma}_2 = \{\begin{smallmatrix} 1 & 1 \\ 1 & 4 \end{smallmatrix}\}$

Equal priors were used and in each case three design set sizes (64, 200, 729) were studied. An independent test set of 500 points gave estimates of misclassification rates. Five methods of analysis were used: Fisher's linear discriminant function, a kernel method with bivariate normal product kernel and a single $h = n^{-1/8}$, a nearest neighbour (k-NN) density estimator classifier (see Sections 6.1 and 7.3 and Hand (1981b)), a classifier derived from an estimator based on statistically equivalent blocks, and a nearest neighbour classifier based on probability squares. The results are reproduced (from Gessaman and Gessaman, 1972, Table 1, with permission) in Table 7.1. As can be seen, in comparison with the other methods Fisher's method performs well on the third set of data (for which $\underline{\Sigma}_1 = \underline{\Sigma}_2$) and less well on the other two sets (for which $\underline{\Sigma}_1 \neq \underline{\Sigma}_2$). This seems to be generally true of Fisher's method: it performs well (even on binary data) if the true decision surface is roughly linear and comparatively poorly otherwise. The kernel method and the k-NN method gave very similar results, as did the kernel method and the probability square method for the first set of data. From the kernel point of view the worst case occurs in the largest sample comparison of the second data set, where the kernel method misclassifies 8.6% more than the probability square method. It would be interesting to see why the kernel method does not perform better in this large sample experiment. Part of the explanation may lie in the choice of the value for h. It

TABLE 7.1

Results of Gessaman and Gessaman's (1972) comparison of five methods of discriminant analysis on three pairs of normal distributions. The table contains misclassification rates.

	(i)			(ii)			(iii)		
n =	64	200	729	64	200	729	64	200	729
Fisher	.112	.118	.116	.498	.496	.502	.166	.158	.150
Kernel	.100	.100	.090	.354	.332	.328	.176	.168	.172
k-NN	.102	.108	.096	.370	.336	.320	.178	.162	.160
Stat. equiv. blocks	.140	.108	.110	.436	.356	.360	.200	.160	.160
Prob. square	.098	.096	.090	.304	.292	.246	.178	.158	.142

would also be interesting to extend the comparison using more sophisticated kernel methods (for example, with different h's in each class and/or dimension).

Goldstein (1975) compares a kernel method, a k-NN density estimation method, and the common parametric approach of replacing each class by a normal distribution. Whereas most comparisons concentrate on the two class case, he studied the five class case where the classes (equal priors) have the following normal distributions:

(i) $\underline{\mu}_1 = (2,0)$ $\underline{\Sigma}_1 = \{\begin{smallmatrix} 1 & 2 \\ 2 & 9 \end{smallmatrix}\}$

(ii) $\underline{\mu}_2 = (0,0)$ $\underline{\Sigma}_2 = \{\begin{smallmatrix} 1 & 1 \\ 1 & 4 \end{smallmatrix}\}$

(iii) $\underline{\mu}_3 = (0,0)$ $\underline{\Sigma}_3 = \{\begin{smallmatrix} 1 & -1 \\ -1 & 4 \end{smallmatrix}\}$

(iv) $\underline{\mu}_4 = (1,1)$ $\underline{\Sigma}_4 = \{\begin{smallmatrix} 1 & 1 \\ 1 & 4 \end{smallmatrix}\}$

(v) $\underline{\mu}_5 = (-1,0)$ $\underline{\Sigma}_5 = \{\begin{smallmatrix} 1 & 1 \\ 1 & 4 \end{smallmatrix}\}$

For each method Goldstein generated design samples of sizes 75, 100, and 150 for each class and 300 point test sets. He gives the results for the case n = 100, stating that "very similar patterns evolved for n = 75 and 150". For the kernel method he used a Rosenblatt product kernel with $h = 0.4\, n^{-\alpha}$ and tried $\alpha = 0$, 0.2, 0.35, 0.5, 0.7. (Note: Goldstein's text gives $\alpha = 0.6$ instead of 0.5, but his two tables give 0.5.) In the k-NN method he set $k = \{n^\beta\}$ with $\beta = 0$, 0.25, 0.5, 0.65, 0.75. (Note: Goldstein's text gives 0.60 where his two tables give

0.65).

The normal method misclassified 165 points, the kernel method misclassified 181, 171, 192, 220 and 237 (in the above order of α), and the k-NN method misclassified 177, 176, 165, 163 and 180 (in the above order of β). For the kernel method h decreases as α increases and we observe a U-shaped curve. Note that the optimum occurs at about $\alpha = \frac{1}{5}$, as suggested in Chapter 3.

It is difficult to draw any general conclusions from so small an experiment - especially in making comparisons between kernel and k-NN methods. Perhaps one, rather negative, conclusion is that any comparison implicitly includes a comparison of the methods used for determining h and k. One point worthy of note, however, is that the normal method - which is optimal for this data - did not do much better than the nonparametric methods.

Van Ness and Simpson (1976) describe a study in which the main aim was to compare the relationship between dimensionality, error rate, and sample size for different types of classifier. They used samples of size n = 10 and 20, and equally probable classes following normal densities with parameters

$$\underline{\mu}_1 = (0,\ldots,0) \qquad \underline{\Sigma}_1 = \underline{I}$$
$$\underline{\mu}_2 = (\mu,0,\ldots,0) \qquad \underline{\Sigma}_2 = \underline{I}$$

Thus the classes have the same population distribution shape but their means are a distance μ apart. Amongst other things the authors presented plots of d against μ for fixed values of the probability of correct classification (set to 0.6, 0.7 and 0.8). These allow one to

see how much extra separation a variable must give in order to be worth
adding.

To summarise the results broadly, the order of the classifiers was
(from requiring least increase in separation to requiring most):

1. linear (normal distributions) with known $\underline{\Sigma}_i = \underline{I}$, i = 1,2,

2. kernel (normal product and Cauchy product kernels were used and
    gave much the same results),

3. linear (normal distributions), but $\underline{\Sigma}_1 = \underline{\Sigma}_2$ not given beforehand,

4. quadratic (normal distributions with $\underline{\Sigma}_1 \neq \underline{\Sigma}_2$, unknown).

The differences become more marked as d increases - which is perhaps
to be expected since n remains constant.

The fact that the linear method with known $\underline{\Sigma}_i$ did best is hardly
surprising. It is ideally matched to the known form of the data and is
not really a practical method. It was merely included as a benchmark.
It is rather surprising that the linear method with unknown $\underline{\Sigma}_1 = \underline{\Sigma}_2$ did
not perform better. Indeed Van Ness and Simpson state that their
expected ordering would have been linear ($\underline{\Sigma}$ known), linear ($\underline{\Sigma}$ unknown),
quadratic, kernel. Kernel coming last because it uses no information
about the shapes of the distributions. The poor linear ($\underline{\Sigma}$ unknown)
performance is probably due to poor covariance matrix estimates as the
d/n ratio increases.

It is also interesting to note that the difference between the kernel
and the linear ($\underline{\Sigma}$ known) methods (i.e. the difference between the
increase in separation required by these methods as variables are
added) does not increase as d increases from about 3 to 20.

There was virtually no difference between the normal and Cauchy kernel results, demonstrating the often reported basic insensitivity of the kernel method to choice of kernel shape.

The astute reader will have noticed that we have made no mention of how the h parameter was selected in this study. As a cautionary note, lest too much weight is put on these results, it should be remarked that the selection of the smoothing parameter was based on additional samples from the same distribution. This gives something of an unfair advantage to the kernel method. Van Ness and Simpson discuss this point and present a graph showing that when h exceeds a certain value the misclassification performance becomes insensitive to the value of h. In view of the nature of the data this is not really surprising: the optimal decision surface is linear and as h increases so the kernel estimate tends more and more to the kernel shape - giving, for these kernels, a linear decision surface. It seems vital to make similar comparisons on data which do not unfairly favour the kernel method in this way.

And this is what Van Ness (1979) has done. He considered two normal populations, as before, but here $\Sigma_1 = I$ and $\Sigma_2 = I/2$. Amongst other classifiers he compared quadratic (known Σ_i, as benchmark), linear (unknown $\Sigma_1 = \Sigma_2$), quadratic (unknown $\Sigma_1 \neq \Sigma_2$), kernel (normal product kernel with same h in each class), and kernel (normal product kernel with different h_i in each class - see Section 3.5). The smoothing parameter was chosen by a jackknife method from the design set.

Plots similar to those of Van Ness and Simpson (1976) were produced. To summarise (and perhaps over-simplify) the results, the order from best to worst was (at least, for d greater than about 5): quadratic (known $\underline{\Sigma}_i$), kernel (different h_i), linear and kernel (same h) about the same, and quadratic (unknown $\underline{\Sigma}_i$). For smaller d the differences between the methods was not so clear. Van Ness observes "in this paper we have found a much greater sensitivity to σ (his spread parameter)" - as we predicted.

The poor performance of the quadratic method for large d is attributed to the fact that the sample covariance matrices are poor estimates with such large d/n ratios. Van Ness concludes: "However, the general conclusion of (9) (Van Ness and Simpson, 1976), that the nonparametric algorithms are quite stable at high dimensions, is strongly supported by the performance of algorithm V (i.e. kernel with different smoothing parameters in each class). The only qualification added by this paper is that the windows must be adapted to the population covariances."

Van Ness (1980) then takes this series of comparisons a stage further by letting the two normal classes have different (diagonal) covariance matrices. In fact

$$\underline{\Sigma}_1 = \underline{I} \qquad \underline{\Sigma}_2 = \left\{ \begin{matrix} \underline{I}_{d/2} & 0 \\ 0 & \frac{1}{2}\underline{I}_{d/2} \end{matrix} \right\}$$

(where $\underline{I}_p$ is the p dimensional identity matrix), $\underline{\mu}_1 = \underline{0}$, $\underline{\mu}_2 = (\mu/2, 0, \ldots, 0, \mu/2)$. Again the classes had equal priors and performance was measured by misclassification rate. Again a normal product kernel was used, only now the smoothing parameter for each variable and class was taken as being proportional to the sample standard deviation for that variable and class (c.f. Remme et al, 1980). The constant of proportionality was determined by a cross validatory method (details in Van Ness, 1980). In view of the fact that the data are generated from normal populations with diagonal covariance matrices this seems, to the present author, to provide a slight bias in favour of the kernel method. Van Ness discusses other possible choices of kernel - and gives a warning about the problems that may be encountered if the $\underline{\Sigma}_j$ are nearly singular.

Once again plots similar to Van Ness and Simpson (1976) are produced for n = 10 and 20. As the dimensionality increases a relative deterioration in the performance of the quadratic algorithm quickly becomes apparent. The linear method does not fall behind the kernel method as quickly, but does when d becomes sufficiently large. Van Ness (1980) also gives plots of the percentage of test points correctly classified by the linear, quadratic, and kernel methods against the percentage classified correctly by the "benchmark" method using the true covariance matrices. The kernel method does not show such a dramatic deterioration as the other methods. Van Ness comments that the most startling result is the superiority of the kernel method in high dimensions.

A further interesting point concerns the choice of the constant of proportionality referred to above. Whereas in Van Ness and Simpson (1976) a gradual deterioration in classification performance was apparent as h increased beyond some threshold level, in Van Ness (1980) the performance falls off quite rapidly as the constant of proportionality increases. A U-shaped curve of misclassification rate against smoothing parameter occurs. In the light of our earlier discussion this is perhaps to be expected.

A more extensive comparison of the normal product kernel method with classical linear and quadratic methods has been made by Remme, Habbema and Hermans (1980). They consider two classes with equal priors, sample sizes of n = 30 and 70 and various d from 2 to 10. Their performance measures are based on test sets of size 50 and are averaged over 25 repetitions of each situation. This is an interesting study because it breaks away from the tradition of simple normal class conditional distributions. They examined:

(i)   normal classes with $\underline{\Sigma}_1 = \underline{\Sigma}_2$

(ii)   normal classes with $\underline{\Sigma}_2 = r\underline{\Sigma}_1 = r\underline{I}$

(iii)   lognormal classes

(iv)   classes which had normal mixture distributions.

This paper is also interesting because it does not use simple error rate as the performance criterion but examines how closely the estimated probability at a test point matches the known true class conditional probability. The measures for which the results are discussed are:

(a) The percentage of test elements for which

   (both $\hat{f}_1(\underline{x})$ and $f_1(\underline{x})$ lie in the range $\{0,.1\}$)

   or (both $\hat{f}_1(\underline{x})$ and $f_1(\underline{x})$ lie in the range $\{.1,.9\}$)

   or (both $\hat{f}_1(\underline{x})$ and $f_1(\underline{x})$ lie in the range $\{.9,.1\}$)

(b)   The percentage of test elements for which

$(\hat{f}_1(\underline{x})$ is in $\{.9,.1\}$ while $f_1(\underline{x})$ is in $\{0,.1\})$

or $(\hat{f}_1(\underline{x})$ is in $\{0,.1\}$ while $f_1(\underline{x})$ is in $\{.9,1\})$.

Remme et al present their results for different values of a separability measure C, defined by the percentage of test elements for which the true posterior probability for the population of origin exceeds 0.9. For some of the different situations studied they give graphs of measure (a) above against C for each of the three classifiers (linear, quadratic, kernel).

The normal product kernel used permits a different h for each class and for each dimension, avoiding an excessive proliferation of parameters by setting

$$h^2_{ij} = k_i \, S^2_{ij} \qquad i = 1,\ldots,c \; ; \; j = 1,\ldots,d \qquad (7.1.1)$$

where S^2_{ij} is the design sample variance of variable j for class i and k_i is a parameter specific to class i. The k_i were estimated by the modified maximum likelihood method.

For data type (i) the linear discriminant function, as expected, did best. The kernel method was good when the classes were not well separated but became worst of the three methods for high degrees of separability. With the unequal covariance matrices of data type (ii) the linear method was worst (unless $r \simeq 1$) and deteriorated rapidly as r increased. This is not surprising. What is a little surprising is that, although the quadratic method exactly matches the distributions it was not always the best method. The kernel method yielded no large errors. Remme et al make the interesting point that the uncorrelated nature of $\underline{\Sigma}_1$ and $\underline{\Sigma}_2$ might favour the kernel method since a normal product (and hence uncorrelated) kernel is used. Some preliminary results with the $\underline{\Sigma}_i$ non-diagonal suggest that, indeed, the performance of the kernel method is degraded when high correlations are present (see Section 2.3).

For the lognormal distributions none of the methods performed very well (perhaps this is not surprising as far as the linear and quadratic methods go) and no method was markedly superior. Habbema, Hermans and Remme (1978), however, have demonstrated that a location dependent smoothing parameter results in a substantial improvement with lognormal distributions (see Section 3.6).

On populations which were normal mixtures of three equiprobable components the kernel method was best, but other normal mixtures led to equivalent results for the three methods.

Some experiments with n increasing to 200 and 400 show the kernel method quickly becoming superior to the other methods on lognormal and normal mixture class conditional distributions. On normal classes with unequal covariance matrices it is not surprising to find that although the kernel method improves it is surpassed by the quadratic method.

Remme et al state in their final discussion: "The performance of the kernel model was better than or about equal to the performance of the other models, except in the simulations with multinormal distributions with equal covariance matrices. It was surprising that the kernel model in relation to the other model showed very good results in problems with relatively small samples."

This favourable small sample comparison has also been commented on by Van Ness and Simpson (1976, p.184): "A commonly heard maxim is that for small samples you must go parametric and keep the number of 'parameters' small. Yet for the larger values of the probability of correct classification, γ and n = 10 or 20 we see that algorithms IV and V (i.e. the kernel algorithms) are already superior at d = 2 or 3."

The comments by Remme et al support the conclusions of Hermans and Habbema (1975) who compared normal distribution methods and the kernel method on two real data sets with large values of n/d. They found the two types of method gave comparable results when the normality assumption was justifiable, but otherwise the kernel method did better.

Habbema and Hermans (1977) are concerned with variable selection for discriminant analysis and the criteria used for such selection. They compared linear discriminant methods and kernel methods, using a normal product kernel with different h's in each class and each dimension as shown in (7.1.1). The real data set in their comparison (they also used an artificial set which we will not discuss here) had 12 classes with 4 points per class and 9 variables. The error rates at each stage of the variable selection process, calculated by the leaving-one-out method, are shown in Figure 7.1.

Specht (1967) also describes a comparative study involving the kernel method. However, his study is rather different from the above because his comparisons are with a new method of his own, based on the kernel method. He calls the new method the "polynomial discriminant function method" (PDM). It is described in Specht (1967a) and briefly in Chapter 6. The data in his comparison consist of 46 measurements on

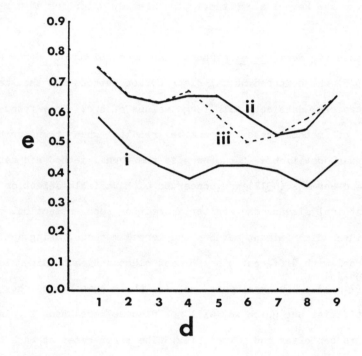

<u>Figure 7.1</u> Leaving-one-out error estimates (e)
as d variables are selected for (i) the kernel
method (ii) the linear method in the BMD/SPSS
programs and (iii) the linear method in the
DISCRIM program.

vectorcardiograms from 224 normal subjects (192 in design set and 32 in test set) and 88 abnormal subjects (57 in design set, 31 in test set). The kernel method used a normal product kernel with equal smoothing in each dimension. This was set to h = 4 on the basis that this produced the greatest accuracy in classifying the design set. The decision threshold was set to misclassify 5% of the normals in the design set. The classification results are shown in Table 7.2, as are those of the polynomial discriminant method derived from this kernel classifier. The reader should be cautioned that the percentages are slightly deceptive in view of the small numbers in the test set. As an aside it is interesting to compare the performance of clinicians (when constrained to use only the information available to the statistical methods) in classifying the test set. This is the last column in Table 7.2.

7.2   CATEGORICAL VARIABLES

Aitken (1978) compares the independence model, a predictive logistic model, and three different kernel methods on binary data. The kernel methods are:

(i)   An Aitchison and Aitken (1976) type product kernel with different λ's for each class but the same in each dimension. These are estimated by the modified maximum likelihood method.

(ii)   A Hills (1967) type kernel.

(iii)   As (i) but with different λ's in each dimension.

TABLE 7.2

The kernel method, the polynomial discriminant method, and the
clinician's scores on the vector cardiographic data test set
(Specht, 1967). The figures show misclassification rates.

| | Kernel | | PDM | | Clinician |
	Design	Test	Design	Test	Test
Normals	.05	.03	.05	.03	.05
Cases	.09	.10	.14	.10	.47

Whereas for continuous variables an obvious choice for a class conditional distributional form is the multivariate normal distribution, for categorical variables the choice is not so obvious. Aitken avoids the problem by studying two real data sets. The first of these is the keratoconjunctivitis sicca (KCS) data described in Anderson et al (1972) and has two classes (n_1 = 40, n_2 = 37) and 10 variables. Equal priors are assumed. The second data set is concerned with thrombosis of the leg and again has two classes (n_1 = 29, n_2 = 36), only now the priors are assumed proportional to design sample size. This data was analysed twice, once with 7 and once with 5 variables.

Error rate was estimated by the leaving-one-out method. On the KCS data the kernel methods did best, with methods (i) and (ii) doing significantly better than method (iii). On the thrombosis data with 7 variables, however, the two non-kernel methods did best - though the order within the kernel methods was the same as on the KCS data. On the thrombosis data with 5 variables, even this pattern breaks down, with methods (i) and (ii) being noticeably worse than (iii). Here the predictive logistic model was best.

Aitken also presents comparisons based on two other measures, one using the reject option (Chapter 6) and one using the average logarithmic separability-measure defined in Section 5.4.

Hand (1982a) presents the results of applying kernel methods and the classical linear discriminant function method to several sets of real binary data (the enuresis data, the 5 and 12 variable psychotropic drug data, and the mental health data described in Chapter 4). From the point of view of comparison between the two types of method two very interesting facts emerge: the kernel method seems to have a much more optimistic apparent error rate than does the linear method, and the true error rate (estimated from independent test sets) seems to be very similar in the two methods. The kernel method used was of a simple type - Aitchison and Aitken (1976) product kernel with an equal smoothing parameter in each dimension (though different in each class). It would be interesting to extend this comparison to other kernel types.

One of the most extensive single comparative studies of discriminant analysis to be published is presented by Titterington et al (1981). They applied a large number of different methods of analysis to four categorical variable sets derived from the records of 1000 patients with severe head injury. Details of the data may be found in Titterington et al (1981) and in the references cited therein . Analytic methods used included independence models, Lancaster models, latent class models, kernel models, normal distribution assumption models, and linear logistic models. Kernels used were the Murray and Titterington (1978) type kernel (see Section 4.2) with unordered categories and marginally chosen parameters, the same assuming ordered categories, the same as the first with multivariate pseudo-Bayes choice of parameters, the same as this assuming ordered categories, marginal and multivariate choices of smoothing parameters treating missing as an extra category, and finally a single smoothing parameter with missing treated as an extra category.

In the comparisons between kernel methods the final one came out as noticeably best. This is perhaps a little surprising as one might have expected methods which permitted different smoothing parameters in each dimension to do best. In the comparisons between method types the kernel performance was disappointing. Titterington et al suggested an explanation for this: "perhaps quite simply because we are trying to be too ambitious in using a discrete kernel approach in this problem. For variable set IV for instance, we are dealing with a contingency table with over 500,000 cells, while imposing very little structure on the cell probabilities. The sparseness of the data can be illustrated by the fact that when, as in KEREX1, KEREX2 and KEREX3, 'missing' is regarded as an extra category, only 37 out of the test set of 500 have feature vectors matching one of the training set. This means that, because of the type of smoothing produced by the kernel method, very small probability estimates are obtained for $\{p(y|\pi_i,D), i = 1,\ldots,k\}$ (the class conditional density function estimates) leading to unreliable $\{p(\pi_i|y,D), i = 1,\ldots,k\}$ (the posterior estimates)".

Titterington et al also comment on the lack of success of the kernel methods with high dimensional data. This is interesting because it conflicts with Van Ness and Simpson (1976), Van Ness (1979) and Van Ness (1980).

7.3   NEAREST NEIGHBOUR METHODS

Kernel estimators with a Rosenblatt kernel are defined by the proportion of the design sample elements which fall in a specified volume of space. More general kernels extend this by relaxing the 0/1 weighting. However, instead of specifying the volume (determined by h) we could define an estimator as being inversely proportional to the volume required to contain a specified proportion of the design set. Estimators based on this principle are termed k-nearest-neighbour (k-NN) estimators. A value for k is chosen and the volume (of a hypersphere, say) centred at $\underline{x}$, the point where we wish to make the estimate, and with radius equal to the distance from $\underline{x}$ to its kth nearest neighbour, is found. Calling this volume V, the density estimate is then given by (k-1)/nV. Just as with kernel estimates h must be chosen, so with k-NN estimates k must be chosen.

When used for classification purposes, straightforward simplifying extensions of the k-NN estimators are possible. For example, we can examine the k nearest neighbours to $\underline{x}$ and classify $\underline{x}$ as belonging to the class which has the majority amongst these nearest neighbours (with appropriate modifications to allow for different priors and costs).

Nearest neighbour estimators are defined in Loftsgaarden and Quesenberry (1965) and both estimators and classifiers are discussed in Hand (1981b).

An interesting property of nearest neighbour methods is that the choice of k is usually relatively uncritical. This should be contrasted with the relative sensitivity of kernel methods (of density estimation, at least) to the choice of h. It has been suggested that the reason for this difference is that the k-NN method is more locally sensitive: in regions in which the population probability density function has a steep slope the kernel method imposes too much smoothing. Whether or not this is the explanation, kernel methods with location dependent smoothing parameters (Section 3.6) avoid this difficulty.

A disadvantage of k-NN methods relative to kernel methods is that by taking, as the radius of the hypersphere, the distance from $\underline{x}$ to a single point (the kth nearest neighbour to $\underline{x}$) one might expect a greater standard deviation of estimate than results from the averaging process of the kernel method. To alleviate this one could take, not simply the distance to the kth nearest neighbour, but instead the averages of distances to the k nearest neighbours and modify the estimator accordingly. In fact one could go even further, and consider all the design sample points for the class in question, weighting them not by 0/1 (1 if amongst the k nearest neighbours to $\underline{x}$, 0 otherwise) but by some smooth function which decays as distance from $\underline{x}$ increases. If we do adopt such an averaging process then the method becomes formally identical to the kernel method with location dependent smoothing parameter.

7.4 CONCLUSION

The kernel method of discriminant analysis is an exciting area of statistics and pattern recognition. It is applicable to problems for which more traditional methods are ill-suited. Despite the fact that it is a relatively young area it has an impressive mathematical pedigree and has been applied in a large number of areas, ranging from nuclear reactor control to psychiatric diagnosis. It is very much a dynamic field, with new papers appearing even as the book was being prepared. Answers to many questions are slowly forming as the body of theoretical, simulation and real data results accumulates, but many

236

other questions remain open and have barely been touched. This means
that it is a rich field for further research.

References

Aitchison, J. and Aitken, C.G.G. (1976). Multivariate binary discrimination by the kernel method, Biometrika, 63, 413-420.

Aitchison, J., Habbema, J.D.F. and Kay, J.W. (1977). A critical comparison of two methods of statistical discrimination, Applied Statistics, 26, 15-25.

Aitken, C.G.G. (1978). Methods of discrimination in multivariate binary data, Compstat 78. Ed. L.C.A. Corsten and J. Hermans. Publ. Physica-Verlag: Vienna.

Anderson, G.D. (1969). A comparison of methods for estimating a probability density function. Unpublished PhD Thesis, University of Washington.

Anderson, J.A., Whaley, K., Williamson, J. and Buchanan, W.W. (1972). A statistical aid to the diagnosis of keratoconjunctivitis sicca, Quarterly J. Med., 41, 175-189.

Bartlett, M.S. (1963). Statistical estimation of density functions, Sankhya, 25A, 245-254.

Bickel, P. and Rosenblatt, M. (1973). On some global measures of the deviations of density function estimates, Ann. Statist., 1, 1071-1095.

Bishop, Y.M.M., Fienberg, S.E. and Holland, P.W. (1975), Discrete multivariate Analysis, MIT Press: Cambridge, Massachusetts.

Boneva, L., Kendall, D. and Stefanov, I. (1971). Spline transformations: three new diagnostic aids for the statistical data-analyst, J. Royal Stat. Soc., B-33, 1-71.

Bowman, A.W. (1980). A note on consistency of the kernel method for the analysis of categorical data. Biometrika, 67, 682-684.

Boyd, D.W. and Steele, M.J. (1978). Lower bounds for nonparametric density estimation rates, Ann. Statist., 6, 932-934.

Breiman, L., Meisel, W. and Purcell, E. (1977). Variable kernel estimates of multivariate densities, Technometrics, 19, 135-144.

Cacoullos, T. (1966). Estimation of a multivariate density, Ann. Inst. Statist. Math., 18, 179-189.

Copas, J.B. and Fryer, M.J. (1980). Density estimation and suicide risks in psychiatric treatment, J. Royal Statist. Soc., (A), 143, 167-176.

De Figueiredo, R.J.P. (1974). Determination of optimal potential functions for density estimation and classification. Proc. 1974 Int. Conf. on Systems, Man and Cybernetics, 335-7.

238

Devroye, L.P. and Wagner, T.J. (1980). Distribution free consistency results in nonparametric discrimination and regression function estimation. Ann. Statist., 8, 231-9.

Dische, S., Yule, W., Corbett, J., Hand, D.J. (1982). Childhood nocturnal enuresis: factors associated with outcome of treatment with an enuresis alarm. In press.

Dubuisson, B. and Lavison, P. (1980). Surveillance of a nuclear reactor by use of a pattern recognition methodology. IEEE Transactions on Systems, Man and Cybernetics, SMC-10, 603-609.

Duda, R. and Hart, P. (1973). Patern classification and scene analysis. Wiley: New York.

Duin, R.P.W. (1976). On the choice of smoothing parameters for Parzen estimators of probability density functions. IEEE Transactions on Computers, C-25, 1175-1179.

Efron, B. (1979). Bootstrap methods: another look at the jackknife, Ann. Statist., 7, 1-26.

Epanechnikov, V.A. (1969). Nonparametric estimates of a multivariate probability density, Theor. Prob. Appl., 14, 153-158.

Everitt, B.S. and Hand, D.J. (1981). Finite mixture distributions, Chapman and Hall: London.

Farrell, R. (1972). On the best obtainable asymptotic rates of convergence in estimation of a density function at a point, Ann. Math. Statist., 43, 170-180.

Fienberg, S.E. and Holland, P.W. (1973). Simultaneous estimation of multinomial cell probabilities. J. Amer. Statist. Assoc., 68, 683-691.

Fix, E. and Hodges, J. (1951). Discriminatory analysis, nonparametric discrimination: consistency properties. Report no. 4, project no. 21-49-004, USAF School of Aviation Medicine, Randolph Field, Texas.

Fryer, M.J. (1976). Some errors associated with the non-parametric estimation of density functions. J. Inst. Maths. Applics., 18, 371-80.

Fryer, M.J. (1977). A review of some non-parametric methods of density estimation, J. Inst. Maths. Applics., 20, 335-354.

Fukunaga, K. (1972) Introduction to statistical pattern recognition, Academic Press, London.

Fukunaga, K. and Kessell, D.L. (1971). Estimation of classification error, IEEE Transactions on Computers, C-20, 1521-1527.

Fukunaga, K. and Narendra, P.M. (1975). A branch and bound algorithm for computing k-nearest neighbours, IEEE Transactions on Computers, C-24, 750-753.

Gessaman, M.P. and Gessaman, P.H. (1972). A comparison of some multivariate discrimination procedures. Journal of the American Statistical Association, 67, 468-472.

Gilbert, E.S. (1968). On discrimination using qualitative variables, J. Amer. Statist. Assoc., 63, 1399-1412.

Glick, N. (1972). Sample based classification procedures derived from density estimators, J. Amer. Statist. Assoc., 67, 116-122.

Goldberg, D.P. (1972). The detection of psychiatric illness by questionnaire, Maudsley Monograph 21, Oxford University Press: London.

Goldstein, M. (1975). Comparison of some density estimate classification procedures, J. Amer. Statist. Assoc., 70, 666-669.

Goldstein, M. and Dillon, W.R. (1978). Discrete Discriminant Analysis, Wiley: New York.

Good, I.J. (1965). The estimation of probabilities, MIT Press: Cambridge, Massachusetts.

Good, I.J. (1967). A Bayesian significance test for multinomial distributions, J. Royal Statist. Soc., B-29, 399-431.

Greblicki, W. (1978). Asymptotically optimal pattern recognition procedures with density estimates. IEEE Transactions on Information Theory, IT-24, 250-251.

Habbema, J.D.F. and Hermans, J. (1977). Selection of variables in discriminant analysis by F-statistic and error rate, Technometrics, 19, 487-493.

Habbema, J.D.F., Hermans, J. and Remme, J. (1978). Variable kernel density estimation in discriminant analysis, Compstat 78, Ed. L.C.A. Corsten and J. Hermans, Publ. Physica-Verlag, Vienna, 178-185.

Habbema, J.D.F., Hermans, J. and van den Broek, K. (1974). A stepwise discriminant analysis program using density estimation, Compstat 74, Ed. G. Bruckman, Vienna: Physica-Verlag, 101-110.

Habbema, J.D.F., Hermans, J. and van der Burgt, A.T. (1974). Cases of doubt in allocation problems, Biometrika, 61, 313-324.

Hall, P. (1981). On nonparametric multivariate binary discrimination, Biometrika, 68, 287-294.

Hall, P. (1981a). Optimal near neighbour estimator for use in discriminant analysis, Biometrika, 68, 572-575.

240

Hand, D.J. (1981). Branch and bound in statistical data analysis, The Statistician, 30, 1-13.

Hand, D.J. (1981a). Statistical pattern recognition on binary features. In Proceedings of the 1981 NATO Advanced Study Institute on Pattern Recognition and Image Processing, Ed. J. Kittler and L. Pau, Publ. D. Reidel: Boston.

Hand, D.J. (1981b). Discrimination and Classification, Wiley: Chichester.

Hand, D.J. (1982a). A comparison of two methods of discriminant analysis on binary data. In press.

Hand, D.J. and Batchelor, B.G. (1978). An edited condensed nearest neighbour rule. Information Sciences, 14, 171-180.

Hart, P.E. (1968). The condensed nearest neighbour rule, IEEE Transactions on Information Theory, IT-14, 515-516.

Hermans, J. and Habbema, J.D.F. (1975). Comparison of five methods to estimate posterior probabilities, EDV in Medizin und Biologie, 6, 14-19.

Hills, M. (1967). Discrimination and allocation with discrete data, Applied Statistics, 16, 237-250.

Johnson, B.M. (1971). On the admissible estimators for certain fixed binomial problems. Ann. Math. Statist., 42, 1579-1587.

Kittler, J. (1975). Mathematical methods of feature selection in pattern recognition. Int. J. Man-Machine Studies, 7, 609-637.

Klecka, W.R. (1980). Discriminant analysis, SAGE Publications Inc., Beverley Hills.

Koontz, W.L.G. and Fukunaga, K. (1972). Asymptotic analysis of a nonparametric clustering technique, IEEE Transactions on Computers, C-21, 967-974.

Krzanowski, W.J. (1977). The performance of Fisher's linear discriminant function under non-optimal conditions, Technometrics, 19, 191-200.

Kullback, S. (1968). Information theory and statistics, Dover Publications: New York.

Lachenbruch, P.A. (1975). Discriminant analysis, Hafner Press: New York.

Loeve, M. (1960). Probability Theory, Van Nostrand: Princeton.

Loftsgaarden, D.O. and Quesenberry, C.P. (1965). A nonparametric estimate of a multivariate density function. Ann. Math. Statist., 36, 1049-1051.

Meisel, S.M. (1972). Computer-oriented approaches to pattern recognition, Academic Press: New York.

Meyer, T.G. (1977). Bounds for estimation of density functions and their derivatives. Ann. Statist. 5, 136-142.

Moore, D.H. (1973). Evaluation of five discrimination procedures for binary variables, J. Amer. Statist. Assoc., 68, 399-404.

Murray, G.D. and Titterington, D.M. (1978). Estimation problems with data from a mixture, Applied Statistics, 27, 325-334.

Murthy, V. (1965). Estimation of probability density, Ann. Math. Statist., 36, 1027-1031.

Nadaraya, E. (1965). On non-parametric estimates of density functions and regression curves, Theor. Probability Appl., 10, 186-190.

Nadaraya, E. (1974). The integral mean square error of certain non-parametric estimates of a probability density (Russian) Teor. Verojatnost. i Primenen, 19, 131-139.

Nie, N.H., Hull, C.H., Jenkins, J.G., Steinbrenner, K., Bent, D.H. (1975). Statistical package for the social sciences, McGraw Hill: New York.

Ojo, M.O. (1974). Unpublished M.Phil Dissertation, University of Essex, England.

Parzen, E. (1962). On estimation of a probability density function and mode, Ann. Math. Statist, 33, 1065-76.

Patrick, E.A. and Fischer, F.P. (1969). Nonparametric feature selection, IEEE Transactions on Information Theory, IT-15, 577-584.

Quesenberry, C.P. and Gessaman, M.P. (1968). Nonparametric discrimination using tolerance regions, Ann. Math. Statist., 39 664-673.

Raatgever, J.W. and Duin, R.P.W. (1978). On the variable kernel model for multivariate nonparametric density estimation, Compstat 78, Ed. L.C.A. Corsten and J. Hermans, Physica-Verlag. Vienna, 524-533.

Rao, C.R. (1951). Advanced statistical methods in biometric research, John Wiley and Sons: New York.

Remme, J., Habbema, J.D.F. and Hermans, J. (1980). A simulative comparison of linear, quadratic and kernel discrimination, J. Statist. Comput. Simul., 11, 87-106.

Rosenblatt, M. (1956). Remarks on some non-parametric estimates of a density function, Ann. Math. Statist., 27, 832-7.

Rosenblatt, M. (1971). Curve estimates, Ann. Math. Statist. , 42, 1815-1842.

Sacks, J. and Ylvisaker, D. (1981). Asymptotically optimum kernels for density estimation at a point. Ann. Statist., 9, 334-336.

Schucany, W.R. and Sommers, J.P. (1977). Improvement of kernel type density estimators, J. Amer. Statist. Assoc., 72, 420-423.

Schuster, R. (1969). Estimation of a probability density function and its derivatives, Ann. Math. Statist., 40, 1187-1195.

Scott, D.W. and Factor, L.E. (1981). Monte Carlo study of three data-based non-parametric probability density estimators, J. Amer. Statist. Assoc., 76, 9-15.

Scott, D.W., Tapia, R.A. and Thompson, J.R. (1977). Kernel density estimation revisited, Journal of nonlinear analysis, theory, methods, and applications, 1, 339-372.

Seheult, A.H. and Quesenberry, C.P. (1971). On unbiased estimation of density functions, Ann. Math. Statist., 42, 1434-1438.

Shanmugam, K. (1977). On a modified form of Parzen estimator for nonparametric pattern recognition, Pattern Recognition, 9, 167-170.

Silverman, B.W. (1978). Weak and strong uniform consistency of the kernel estimate of a density of its derivatives, Ann. Statist., 6, 177-184.

Silverman, B.W. (1978a). Choosing the window width when estimating a density, Biometrika, 65, 1-11.

Shapiro, J.S. (1969). Smoothing and approximation of functions, Van Nostrand Reinhold: New York.

Smith, A.F.M. and Makov, U.E. (1978). A quasi-Bayes sequential procedure for mixtures, J.Royal Statist. Soc., B-39, 44-47.

Specht, D.F. (1967). Vectorcardiographic diagnosis using the polynomial discriminant method of pattern recognition. IEEE Transactions on Bio-medical Engineering, BME-14, 90-95.

Specht, D.F. (1967a). Generation of polynomial discriminant functions for pattern recognition, IEEE Transactions on Electronic Computers, EC-16, 308-319.

Stone, M. (1974). Cross-validatory choice and assessment of statistical predictions, J. Royal Statist. Soc., B-36, 111-147.

Stone, M. (1974a). Cross-validation and multinomial prediction, Biometrika, 61, 509-515.

Tapia, R.A. and Thompson, J.R. (1978). Nonparametric probability density estimation. John Hopkins University Press: Baltimore.

Titterington, D.M. (1976). Updating a diagnostic system using unconfirmed cases, Applied Statistics, 25, 238-247.

Titterington, D.M. (1977). Analysis of incomplete multivariate binary data by the kernel method, Biometrika, 64, 455-460.

Titterington, D.M. (1980). A comparative study of kernel-based density estimates for categorical data, Technometrics, 22, 259-268.

Titterington, D.M., Murray, G.D., Murray, L.S., Spiegelhalter, D.J., Skene, A.M., Habbema, J.D.F., Gelpke, G.J. (1981). Comparison of discrimination techniques applied to a complex data set of head injured patients. J. Royal Statist. Soc., Series A, 144, 145-174.

Tou, J.T. and Gonzalez, R.C. (1974). Pattern recognition principles, Addison-Wesley: Reading, Mass.

Toussaint, G.T. (1974). Bibliography on estimation of misclassification, IEEE Transactions on Information Theory, IT-20, 472-479.

Vaduva, I. (1963). Estimation of a density of distribution in K-dimensions (Romanian) Acad. R.P. Romine Stud. Cerc. Mat., 14, 653-660.

Vaduva, I. (1968). Contributions to the theory of statistical estimation of probability density functions and its applications (Romanian). Stud. Cerc. Mat., 20, 1207-1276.

Van Ness, J.W. and Simpson, C. (1976). On the effects of dimension in discriminant analysis, Technometrics, 18, 175-187.

Van Ness, J. (1979). On the effects of dimension in discriminant analysis for unequal covariance matrices, Technometrics, 21, 119-127.

Van Ness, J. (1980). On the dominance of non-parametric Bayes rule discriminant algorithms in high dimensions. Pattern Recognition, 12, 355-368.

Van Ryzin, J. (1966). Bayes risk consisting of classification procedures using density estimation, Sankhya, Series A, 261-270.

Victor, N. (1980). Medical diagnostics with nonparametric allocation rules, Metamedicine, 1, 85-94.

Van Ryzin, J. (1969). On strong consistency of density estimates, Ann. Math. Statist., 40, 1765-1772.

244

Wagner, T.J. (1975). Nonparametric estimates of probability densities, IEEE Transactions on Information Theory, IT-21, 438-440.

Wahba, G. (1975). Optimal convergence properties of variable knot, kernel and orthogonal series methods for density estimation, Ann. Statist., 3, 15-29.

Wang, M.C. and Van Ryzin, J. (1981). A class of smooth estimators for discrete distributions, Biometrika, 68, 301-309.

Watson, G. and Leadbetter, M. (1963). On the estimation of the probability density I, Ann Math. Statist., 34, 480-491.

Wegman, E.J. (1972). Nonparametric probability density estimation: I. A summary of available methods, Technometrics, 14, 533-546.

Wertz, W. (1978). Statistical density estimation: A survey, Vandenhoeck and Ruprecht: Gottingen.

Wertz, W. and Schneider, B. (1979). Statistical density estimation: a bibliography, International Statistical Review, 47, 155-175.

Woodroofe, M. (1970). On choosing a delta-sequence, Ann. Math. Statist., 41, 1665-1671.

Yamato, H. (1972). Some statistical properties of estimators of density and distribution functions, Bull. Math. Statist., 19, 113-131.

Young, T.Y. and Calvert, T. (1974). Classification, estimation and pattern recognition, American Elsevier, New York.